Phebe's Hitchin Book

Memories of Life in Regency Hitchin

By Phebe Glaisyer

Transcribed and annotated by John Lucas

A Hitchin Historical Society Publication

A Hitchin Historical Society Publication 2009
http://www.hitchinhistoricals.org.uk

© Copyright Hitchin Historical Society and John Lucas

ISBN: 978-0-9552411-4-7

Design and layout: Barrie Dack and Associates 01462 834640
Printed by: Olive Press, Stotfold, Hitchin, Herts, 01462 733333

Cover illustration:	The River Hiz from a watercolour by Margaret Thompson (1843-1928), a second cousin of Phebe Lucas. The Lucas Brewery is shown on the left of the painting — Hitchin Museum.
Inside front cover:	An 1820 map showing the Hitchin that Phebe would have known in her childhood. It was printed in Robert Clutterbuck's *The History and Antiquities of the County of Hertford,* (Vol Three) published in London c1827. The map was the contribution of William Wilshere in a form of a sponsorship — Hitchin Museum.
Half title page:	A silhouette of Phebe Glaisyer — Reproduced from *Hitchin Worthies* by Reginald Hine.
Frontispiece:	Baldock and Hitchin Monthly Meeting Friends' register for the years 1815 to 1818. It records Phebe's birth and several others whose names are to be found in her journal, including Joseph Whiting, Eliza Marsh, Francis Lucas, Joshua Whiting and Joseph Ransom.
Inside rear cover:	An original page from Phebe's journal – Hitchin Museum.
Rear cover:	The Lucas Brewery in 1913, some 10 years before it closed. From a watercolour by Alice Mary Lucas – Hitchin Museum. Photograph – The author, John Lucas.

Phebe's Hitchin Book

When Born.	Where Born.	Name.	Son or Daughter.	Names of Parents.	Residence.	Description of the Father.
12th day of the 2nd Month — 1815	Hitchin in the parish of Hitchin County of Herts	Joseph Whiting	Son	John Whiting & Margaret his Wife	Hitchin	Fellmonger
2nd day of the 2nd Month 1816	Hitchin in the parish of Hitchin County of Herts	Eliza Martha	Daughter	Thomas Marsh & Mary Hanna & Maria his Wife	Hitchin	
2nd day of the 7th Month — 1816	Baldock in the parish of Baldock County of Herts	Edward Morris	Son	Joseph Morris & Martha his Wife	Ampthill	Brewer
29th day of the 4th Month 1815	Cranmore in the parish of Cranmore County of Hereford	Rachel Christy	Daughter	Miller Christy & Ann his Wife	Gosmore	Not a member of the Society of Friends Hatt Maker
1st day of the 6th Month 1816	Hitchin in the parish of Hitchin County of Herts	James Francis & Henry Lucas	two Sons	William Lucas junior & Ann his Wife —	Hitchin	Brewer —
3rd day of the 5th Month 1816	Ashwell in the parish of Ashwell County of Herts	Mary Kitchener	Daughter	William Kitchener & Sarah his Wife	Ashwell	Not a member of the Society of Friends
31st day of the 5th Month 1815	Ampthill in the parish of Ampthill County of Bedford	Eliza Rebecca Pumphrey	Daughter	Thomas Pumphrey & Mary his Wife	Ampthill	
22nd day of this 3rd Month — 1816	Baldock in the parish of Baldock County of Herts	Emily Benson	Daughter	Robert Benson & Hannah his Wife	Baldock	
26 day of the 8th Month — 1816	Hitchin in the parish of Hitchin County of Herts	Phebe Lucas	Daughter	Joseph Lucas & Hannah his Wife	Hitchin	Brewer
8 day of the 3rd Month 1817	Hitchin in the parish of Hitchin in the County of Herts	Joshua Whiting	Son	John Whiting & Margaret his Wife	Hitchin	Fellmonger
22 day of the 9th Month 1817	Baldock in the parish of Baldock in the County of Herts	George Thomas	Son	John Whiting & Margaret his Wife	Baldock	Cooper...
2nd day of the 5th Month 1817	Hitchin in the parish of Hitchin	Joseph Ransom	Son	John Ransom & ... his Wife	Hitchin	Mealsman
15 day of the 1st Month 1818	Baldock in the parish of Baldock	Caroline Morris	Daughter	Joseph Morris & Martha his Wife	Ampthill	Brewer

Contents

Acknowledgements..iii

Introduction..iv

Foreword...v

Plan of central Hitchin....................................vi

Chapter 1 Setting the Scene
      – Regency England..............................1

Chapter 2
      The Quaker Movement....................5

Chapter 3
      The Lucas Brewery...........................14

Chapter 4 – Two Further Hitchin
      Locations
      West Mill..23
      The Lucas property in Cock
      Street (High Street)........................25

Chapter 5 – Recollections of my
      Childhood, the transcript............29

Chapter 6 – Biographical Details 68

Appendix A – The Descent of the
      Lucas Family....................................90

Appendix B – Phebe Family Trees
      1 to 6................................91 – 97

Appendix C – The Will of Joseph Lucas
      (Phebe's Father)..............................98

Sources and Recommended
      Reading...100

Index
     102

"Sheep Shearing" an oil painting by Samuel Lucas, 1845.
In the possession of the author — I was very pleased to have obtained this painting from an internet auction site in 2004.

Acknowledgements

I would like to thank the following people and organisations for their
valuable assistance in the preparation of this book.

David Hodges and his staff at Hitchin Museum, who did so much to make
this book a reality, and in particular for recognising the logistical problems
of carrying out research on brief visits from the other side of the country
and doing all that they could to assist with this.

Christine Low and Matthew Philpott, of Philpott Furnishers in Sun
Street, who have given their enthusiastic support to the project and who
welcomed us so warmly on a visit to Phebe's Brewery House, which has
now been owned by the Philpott family for 72 years.

To Jane Lucas in Vancouver, who is the only Lucas descendant that I
have met who is not in my near family, and who has provided so much
information about the family, particularly in the early days of my research.

David Hitchin, the author of *Quakers in Lewes* and who kindly reviewed the
manuscript and corrected some of my misunderstandings of the
Quaker movement.

Mill Hill School for kindly allowing me to use the photograph of Percy
Lucas on page 79 and the Tate Gallery for allowing reproduction of
'*Harmony In Grey and Green — Miss Cicely Alexander*' on page 64.

Barrie Dack for his great expertiese and assistance in converting my computer
ramblings into a viable product.

Hitchin Historical Society members, Bridget and David Howlett, Phil Rowe,
Derek Wheeler MBE, Pauline Humphries and Scilla Douglas:

Bridget and David, for providing some much needed early guidance on the
form of the book and for reviewing the manuscript. I am also extremely
grateful to Bridget for supplying some valuable historical material
concerning the Lucas Brewery, West Mill and Hitchin Friends Burial
Ground.

Phil, for providing me with a list of Hitchin Friends' burial records back
in 2006.

Derek for his companionship on my visits to Hitchin, his interesting and
amusing anecdotes, for reviewing my manuscript and for readily agreeing
to write the Foreword.

I find it difficult to adequately express my admiration for Scilla and Pauline.
They work so hard for the Society, but have found time to patiently and
expertly guide me through this project and to look after me on my various
visits to Hitchin and make those visits so enjoyable!

Last, but not least, I would like to thank some of my own family; my first
cousin Kevin Rowe, who is also a Lucas descendant, for providing some
family material and photographs. Also, my sister Heather and brother-
in-law Robin Higgs OBE, for reviewing the manuscript and for their
enthusiastic support for the project.

John Lucas, 2009

INTRODUCTION

It was just a few years ago that I became aware of my Hitchin family connections and one of my first 'Hitchin' purchases was Reginald Hine's *Hitchin Worthies*. I found the short chapter on Phebe Glaisyer, my great, great, great aunt, both compelling and intriguing, and was delighted to later find that her manuscript was reposing safely in the treasure trove that is Hitchin Museum. She was born into the Quaker Lucas brewing family in the Brewery House in Sun Street on the 26th of the 8th month, 1816. She married Thomas Glaisyer of Brighton at Hitchin Friends' Meeting house in 1844 and then settled in Brighton with him. They had seven children and 20 grandchildren and for their sake she set down in 1890 her childhood experiences of life in Hitchin and also in Sussex. Hine wrote that *"It ought to be printed in full"* and with this I fully concur. This precious manuscript was known in her family as *The Hitchin Book*, and in the words of Hine *"...gives a gracious account of middle-class Quaker life in the town in the eighteen twenties and thirties."*

Phebe's manuscript (I do hope that she will forgive the 21st century informality in my form of address), a simple household notebook of 104 pages, was acquired by the museum in 1981 from Charles Clayton, who was a descendant of Phebe. She had an excellent hand and transcription of her handwriting proved to be very straightforward. A page of the manuscript is shown inside the rear cover of this book.

Without wishing to detract from Phebe's recollections which are, after all, the *raison d'être* for this book, some introductory chapters have been included to set the scene for the time of her birth, and to provide some additional information about the Quaker movement and some Hitchin locations which are so important to her story. I needed little excuse to make multiple visits to Hitchin, but undertaking the research for the book has given me the pleasurable opportunity to look in some depth at the Lucas family, the brewery and *Sleepy Hollow*, as Hitchin is sometimes affectionately called. I am not a Quaker and had little knowledge of the movement before starting on this project. I did, however, become fascinated by their story and am pleased to offer a brief introduction to the movement here. I do hope that Quakers who read this will not be too troubled by this outsider's view of the Society.

Finally in this introduction, an explanation of a few conventions used throughout the book:

- For eight generations the Lucas's named their eldest son William. To aid identification, any reference to William Lucas also shows the numerical suffix as set out in *The Descent of the Lucas Family* at Appendix A on page 90.
- From the earliest days, Quakers would not use day and month names which had *heathen* origins and accordingly identified them numerically. This convention has been used herein for dates derived from Quaker sources. More information about the Quaker Calendar can be found on the Friends Library web site at *www.quaker.org.uk/library*.

FOREWORD

Over the years it has been my pleasure whilst working for North Herts District Council's Museums service to have access to the many diaries and documents which are kept in the Hitchin Museum Archive. My long-term task was to make manila envelopes or boxes as protective covers for every precious literary relic in the collection. Whilst doing this work professionally, I was also reading them with great interest myself. There are many Lucas documents and letters and each is a treasure trove waiting to be revealed to modern eyes. John Lucas has done just that; his illustrious family history was, until comparatively recently, unknown to him. Whilst those of us who are natives are familiar with the Town Hall's Lucas Room, Samuel Lucas School and Lucas Lane, John Lucas has come but recently into our Hitchin Historical circle and a worthy contribution he has made to our local heritage by opening up the Regency world of his ancestor Phebe Glaisyer, née Lucas!

It has been a privilege to have been asked to contribute to this delightful book and an honour to know John Lucas.

Derek Wheeler MBE

Hitchin Historical Society

On a 'field trip' to the Brewery House in February 2009. Left to right — Derek Wheeler MBE, Matthew Philpott, Scilla Douglas, Christine Low (née Philpott), Pauline Humphries. Photographed by the author.

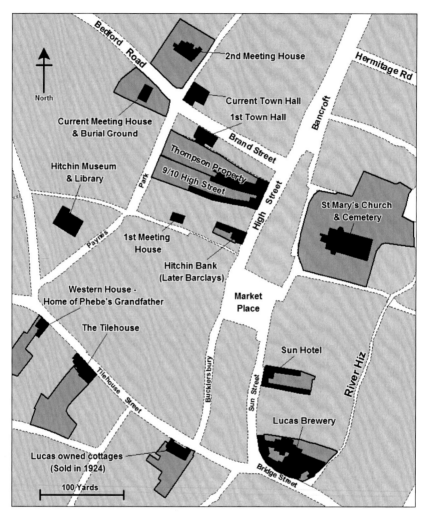

A plan of central Hitchin, showing some of the more significant buildings in the town and this book. Based on the 1915 Ordnance Survey 1:2500 scale map with later additions. (All property boundaries are approximate.)
Prepared by the author.

Chapter 1

Setting the Scene

As Phebe's descriptions of people and events in her childhood years are so vivid, it is worth remembering how long ago and how different were the times of her early years.

She was born into Regency England, 193 years ago. The monarch was *mad* King George (George III) but because of his illness his son (later George IV) was acting as Prince Regent. It would be more than twenty years before Victoria's coronation. Phebe was born less than a year after the Battle of Waterloo and the threat of a French invasion, which had been the stuff of children's nightmares for many years, was finally removed [1]. The end of the war, however, brought huge problems in its wake. Many thousands of soldiers and sailors had returned to the home country, thereby increasing the scarcity of food and employment. The cost of the war had been immense and the economy was in ruins. The plight of the poor had been compounded by the 1815 'Corn Law' (the Importation Act), an import tariff designed to maintain the value of home-grown cereals, but it led to widespread famine and riots in London and, notoriously, the 'Peterloo' massacre in Manchester in 1819 [2]. The period between 1815 and 1822 was accordingly one of the most difficult and troubled in British economic and social history and has been referred to in Britain as *The Long Depression* (In the USA, *The Long Depression* occurred later in the 19th century). It is worth recounting the following from *Plight of the Unemployed 1816* by the social reformer Robert Owen [3]:

"On the day peace was signed, this great customer [The War Machine] died, and prices fell as the demand diminished. … The want of demand compelled master producers to

---

[1] William Lucas VI wrote of his childhood *"When sitting round the fire of an evening our servants would so terrify us with reports of the French having landed on our coast that we were afraid to go to bed".*

[2] The Peterloo Massacre (or Battle of Peterloo) occurred at St Peter's Field, Manchester, on 16 August 1819, when a crowd of 60,000–80,000 gathered at a protest meeting. 15 people were killed and 400–700 were injured when cavalry charged into the crowd with sabres drawn. The massacre was given the name Peterloo in ironic comparison to the Battle of Waterloo, which had taken place four years earlier.

[3] Robert Owen 1771-1858 — his followers were said to be the first "Socialists". He is regarded as being the founder of both the Trade Union and Co-operative movements.

diminish their productions and the cost of producing. Every economy was resorted to, and men being more expensive, they were discharged, and machines made to supersede them."

To further add to the problems, the summer of 1816 was very wet and cold and the harvest failed. The bad weather also caused a potato famine in Ireland (not to be confused with the great potato famine of the 1840s). The poor summer had been caused by a huge volcanic event [4] in The East Indies (Indonesia), in the preceding year.

Even as late as 1825, in a move which has echoes in current times, leading citizens of Hitchin felt compelled to publish a resolution in support of the town's banks. The Revd. Henry Wiles, vicar of St. Mary's, and 90 others, signed the following resolution: *"That we have the fullest confidence in the stability and means of the Banking Houses in this Town and will support their credit to the utmost of our power, and hope by so doing to remove the groundless alarms of the timid, and to preserve this neighbourhood from the unreasonable panic which has been the cause of so much distress in other parts of the country".*

Phebe was, then, very fortunate to have been born into a middle class family which, no doubt, had been affected by the depression but had the financial resources to endure it.

In 1816, the population of Britain was about 17 millions. Very high infant and child mortality rates had remained more or less at the same levels for some 200 years, measles, whooping cough and typhus [5] being particularly prevalent at the time of Phebe's birth. Very few families were unaffected and most suffered the death of at least one child. Phebe's aunt and uncle, Ann & William Lucas V, lost four of their eleven children, two at least to measles, and their son (William VI) recorded that his sister Rachel had been seriously ill with typhus when at school at Doncaster but she thankfully recovered. Phebe's own parents lost one child, Sarah, their firstborn. As Phebe grew older, cholera became a major health problem. A melancholy diary entry by William Lucas V, dated 10th mo 28th 1833, records that *"This town having been long favoured to be free of ye cholera, is so no longer, 3 young subjects being now dead of that disorder, one of Joshua Osborn abt.18 who had worked for us a few years. He took his wages on ye 26th and is now a corpse. Ye others were children".*

Despite these natural constraints upon population growth, Hitchin doubled in size in the first half of the nineteenth century, from just over three thousand in 1801 to more than six thousand in 1841. The 1821 census shows the population of the town to be just under four and a half thousand.

---

[4] On April 10, 1815, the Tambora volcano burst into life on the island of Sumbawa. It was the largest explosive eruption since the beginning of recorded history and is estimated to have directly or indirectly killed over 100,000 people. The eruption caused an atmospheric veil around the Earth, which led to global cooling so severe that in Europe and North America, 1816 was known as "the year without summer".

[5] Typhus mainly killed people living in poor sanitary conditions. It was also a common disease in prisons and for this reason was also known as gaol fever. The typhus bacillus was first identified in 1880 and can now be successfully treated with antibiotics.

The Kershaw Coach – London to Hitchin in just over four hours. It last ran in 1850 when the railway to Hitchin was completed.
From an engraving by Charles Hunt, [6] published in November 1850, — Hitchin Museum.

The Regency period fell in the middle of the first industrial revolution [7] but land transport was still very much dependent on the horse. A viable steam locomotive had been constructed in 1810 but the first public passenger railway, the Stockton & Darlington, did not open until 1825 and it was not until 1850 that Hitchin Station was opened by the Great Northern Railway. The various journeys that Phebe mentions would have been by private horse and carriage or mail coach. Kershaw provided a public coach service between *The Swan,* in Market Place at Hitchin, and Smithfield in London, but the journey took in excess of four hours. The Kershaw coach was withdrawn as soon as the through rail service was opened to Hitchin in 1850.

Finally, to complete this glimpse of 1816, in culture and the arts, Beau Brummell [8], dandy, and ex-friend of the Prince Regent, fled to France to escape debts and was effectively exiled there. Another self-imposed exile from 1816 was Lord Byron, who escaped scandal to live in Genoa and then Greece for

---

[6]   Charles Hunt (b.1806) – A London based engraver who specialised in sporting and coaching scenes.

[7]   Opinions differ on the actual time span, but it could be considered to cover the last quarter of the 18th century and the first half of the 19th.

[8]   Beau Brummell 1778-1840, was the arbiter of men's fashion in Regency England and was once a close friend of the Prince Regent but they had a famous 'falling out'. Brummell is credited with introducing and establishing as fashion the modern man's suit, worn with a tie. His style of dress was known as dandyism and he claimed to take five hours to dress, recommending that boots be polished with champagne. Brummell died in France in poverty, having never returned to England.

the eight remaining years of his life [9]. Also, the Elgin Marbles were purchased by the British Museum; Constable was creating his work *Flatford Mill*, to be completed the following year; Jane Austen's novel *Emma* had been published in December 1815 and Nash had recently started the redesign and rebuilding of the Royal Pavilion at Brighton for the Prince Regent.

---

[9]   William Lucas VI records the return of Lord Byron's body to London in 1824: "The remains of Lord Byron were unloaded opposite John Harris' Wharf and Sam's [Samuel Lucas] fellow apprentice saw the body, looking beautiful in death, taken out of a cask of spirits".

Cock Street Hitchin, Herts.

Cock Street in 1840. One of the original gas lamps can be seen. The Hitchin gas company was formed in 1833 and gas lighting was introduced to the town in 1834. Also in view is the Swan Inn, starting point for the Kershaw coach. The site of the Swan is now occupied by Hitchin Arcade. Reproduced from The History of Hitchin.

Chapter 2

The Religious Society of Friends

Also known as Quakers

The family into which Phebe was born had been in the Quaker movement from almost its earliest origins, a century and a half before. As early as 1658, John Lucas of Hitchin had been incarcerated in the Fleet Prison for his dissident beliefs and it was in a Lucas house that the first Hitchin Meetings were held.

ORIGINS OF THE MOVEMENT

Quakerism had its beginnings in the North of England. It was based on the personal insights of George Fox (1624-1691) who was born in Drayton-in-the-Clay, Leicestershire and became a shoemaker. Between 1643 and 1647, he experienced his own religious conversion to find the *"inner light"* within himself.

From his early experiences, Fox developed a new set of religious values based on the idea that all men were equal in the spirit of God. In 1647 he had a revelation that *"There is an inward light that speaks to each man directly"*. This seemingly simple message forms the basis of the Quaker ethos as it dispenses with the need for an established church and official clergy. A group of like-minded people could meet in silent worship, waiting on God — their synergy as a group being more likely to make His presence felt — instead of filling the time with prayers, sermons and hymns. Fox travelled the country, spreading his message. As early as 1643 and before his ideas were fully formed, he is known to have spoken to a group of Hitchin soldiers, garrisoned at Newport Pagnell, they having *"listened amazed at his outpourings"* according to Hine. The formal birth of the movement is considered to have taken place in 1652 when 1000 people met near Sedbergh (now in Cumbria). In 1655 Fox was in Hertford where he reported *"fine meetings"*, and also at Baldock in the same year.

Intolerance, Persecution and Organisation

These early stirrings of the movement took place at the very time that the Puritan established church was becoming increasingly intolerant of dissent under the authority of Cromwell's Commonwealth Government, although Fox met Cromwell on four occasions and there was said to be a degree of rapport between them. The law required that all citizens attend the established church; pay tithes to the church (this usually equated to one tenth of one's income); refrain from attending religious meetings other than those of the established church; and to swear an oath of allegiance.

Quakers would do none of these things. More trivial infringements were also used to harass them, including failure to doff one's hat to a *person of authority*. Various sanctions were used to punish these 'crimes' including distraint (seizure) of goods, excommunication (seemingly a paradox, but it removed all protection under the law) and imprisonment. In spite of these sanctions, the movement grew and it is estimated that there may have been between thirty and forty thousand Friends in England in 1660.

The authorities became increasingly concerned about the growth of the movement. In Hitchin in 1656, Ralph Radcliffe, son of the owner of The Priory wrote *"The Quakers are growing numerous and troublesome"*. John Bunyan [10], at Bedford, was fiercely anti-Quaker and attacked the *"delusive pernicious doctrine of those unstable souls, the Quakers"*. Despite hopes to the contrary, persecution of Quakers continued until well after the Restoration of the Monarchy in 1660. In 1662 a special Quaker Act decreed that Friends would be transported after a third conviction for attending a Quaker meeting.

In spite of this harassment, Fox saw the way forward as being to strengthen the organisation as a closely-knit, coherent body. He organised a system where local Weekly (or Preparative) Meetings were represented at Monthly Meetings; a group of Monthly Meetings formed a Quarterly Meeting and at the top of the structure was the Yearly Meeting. Inevitably there has been much reorganisation of meetings but the basic structure survives to this day. Women were held to be spiritually equal to men and attended the same religious meetings but, until the end of the 19th century, held separate business meetings. The structure placed a considerable administrative burden upon the Meetings, with appointed representatives reporting back the results of attended meetings, both up and down the hierarchy, and all was faithfully recorded.

A Quaker Meeting circa 1800, from an original drawing by C. E. Brock. Reproduced from The History of Hitchin.

From the earliest days of the movement, births, marriages and deaths of Friends were recorded, together with resignations and 'disownments' (see page 75 for an example of a disownment), and also the transfer of individuals between Meetings; the character of a transferring member was always investigated before being accepted into the 'receiving' Meeting. The

[10] John Bunyan (1628 – 1688) a Puritan and Baptist preacher, famous for writing The Pilgrim's Progress. He was much persecuted for his non-conformist beliefs.

minute books of the business meetings, which recorded these events, are now a fascinating and valued resource for genealogists and historians.

The Hertfordshire Monthly Meeting was established in 1668 and the first Yearly Meeting was held in London in the same year. Meetings were held covertly at Friends' houses, the first in Hitchin being at the house of William Lucas I, at what is now no 9/10 High Street. Despite the secrecy, the authorities were well aware of the meetings and an arrangement was made with the Town Constables to use a barn at the rear of the building as a clearing house for goods taken from the Friends in distraint!

RELAXATION OF THE LAW

Between 1662 and 1673, Charles II, who had Catholic inclinations and was sympathetic towards non-conformists and dissenters, issued three *Declarations of Indulgence* to suspend all penal laws against *"whatsoever sort of nonconformists or recusants"*, but each of these was blocked by Parliament. However, in some cases, the law actually started to act to the benefit of Quakers. In 1683, the first Meeting House in Hertford was illegally pulled down by a group of local notables, including Sir Ralph Radcliffe of Hitchin, but they were made to pay compensation to *"build a larger Conventicle than the one they had destroyed"*. Thereafter there was no interference with Quaker Meetings at Hertford, Baldock or Hitchin.

In 1686, under James II, the *General Pardon* saw the release of some 490 imprisoned Friends under a Royal Warrant and at last, in 1689, during the reign of William & Mary, the *Toleration Act* allowed freedom of worship for all Protestant Non-Conformists, providing that places of worship were registered but dissenters (including Quakers) were barred from public office and the principal universities. They remained legally obliged to pay church rates (and continued to refuse to do so!) until the law was abolished by Gladstone in 1868. The bar on dissenter entrance to the universities was lifted in 1871.

Matilda Lucas [11], recalling her early life in Tilehouse Street in Hitchin (her memories would have been of the 1850s/1860s), told Reginald Hine of the regular ritual of distraint. *'I remember men coming to distrain for church rates. They knew which cupboard to go to, and what to take. In the afternoon it was bought back from Gatward* [12]*"*. Matilda later recalled that she thought that it was a soup ladle which had always been taken.

Hostility towards the dissenters by some sectors of the community continued into the 19th century. In Hitchin, on bonfire night in 1815, an effigy of a Quaker

---

[11]   Matilda Lucas 1849-1943, a daughter of Samuel Lucas (Snr). She lived for thirty years in Rome with her sister Ann. Neither was married. When nearly 90, Matilda wrote Two Englishwomen in Rome, 1871-1900, assisted by Reginald Hine and E.V. Lucas, published in 1938. On a visit to their Elizabethan manor house at Stanegarth in Westmorland in 1930, Hine recorded Matilda's reminiscences of her early years in Hitchin, several references to which are made in this book.

[12]   Gatwards: jewellers, silversmiths and clockmakers, established in 1760 and still trading at their premises in Market Place, Hitchin.

was burned alongside Guy Fawkes in resentment of the unpatriotic citizens *"whose hearts had ne'er within them burned"*, at the famous victory at Waterloo and stones were hurled through the windows of the Meeting House in Quakers' Alley.

HITCHIN MEETING HOUSES AND BURIAL GROUNDS

The first Hitchin Meeting House was built in 1694 in Cod-Piece Alley, which became Quakers' Alley and is now West Alley. This would have been the Meeting House attended by Phebe in her early years. The site is the location of the car park behind Barclays Bank.

An un-attributed newspaper clipping in the Lawson Thompson scrapbook in Hitchin Museum records that *"The present Meeting House [the 2nd] was built in 1839, and is situate at the top of Brand Street, on a piece of ground given by the late Joseph Sharples, Esq. On the opposite side of the road is the Burying Ground, which was first used for that purpose about the year 1718, and the brick wall built around it in 1725. Previous to the year 1718 the funerals of the Society of Friends at Hitchin and the surrounding villages took place in a Burying Ground at St. Ibbs... and upwards of two hundred and twenty bodies are interred in this ground"*. Information provided by Bridget Howlett, [13] from research of the Hitchin Manor Court Book in the National Archives, records that in 1723 a plot of one rood (¼ acre) at Salter's Dell was conveyed to the Quakers for a burial ground for the use of Joseph Sanders, John Kilby (Snr & Jnr), Henry Hobbs, John Draper, William

Hobbs, William Lucas, John Turner and Joseph Ransom and their heirs.

The first burial shown in available records is that of Thomas Kent in 1757. Metford Robson [14] reports *"a series of initialled and named bricks appearing to date from 1726 is built into a boundary wall on the North West side"* and are possibly memorials for earlier burials. It was not until 1850 that a proposition to allow headstones in Quaker Burial Grounds was

Hitchin Friends' Burial Ground which contains headstones bearing the names of many prominent Hitchin families of the 18th and 19th centuries. Photographed in 2006 by the author.

agreed at the Yearly Meeting, so those for earlier burials were created retrospectively. Records for Hitchin Burial Ground show that a total of 350 people were interred

[13] Bridget Howlett: local historian, professional archivist and a leading member of Hitchin Historical Society.

[14] Hitchin Quakers Ancient & Modern: A transcript of a talk by Metford Robson, given to Hitchin Historical Society in November 2002.

The original Meeting House in Quaker's Alley with (probably) Joshua Whiting (1820-1909) [15] (Date Unknown) — Hitchin Museum.

there, the last in a confirmed location being Ida Mary Lucas in 1964. She was Phebe's great-niece, a descendant of both Joseph Lucas (Snr) and Samuel Allen. Ida died, unmarried, at the age of 95 (she is shown in Phebe's family tree on page 95). Four more burials are recorded, the last being in 1983, but their location in the Burial Ground is unknown. There are also four 1990s memorials attached to the north wall.

Construction of the new Meeting House (the 2nd), which had a capacity of 200 worshipers, was completed at a total cost of £2115-19s, much higher than the original estimate of £1200. The sale of the first building raised £717 and the balance was funded by subscriptions from Hitchin Meeting members. Upon completion, the original building was used for housing and was finally demolished in 1960.

On 4th mo 16th 1839 William Lucas V remarked *"Some progress has been made towards building a new meeting house."* In the following year there was cause for celebration when the first wedding in the new Meeting House took place. He wrote (in his usual dry manner!): 12th mo 3rd 1840 *"Edward Latchmore and Esther Whiting were married being the first in our new meeting house".*

At its lowest ebb, the Hitchin Meeting sold the 2nd Meeting House to Hitchin Rural District Council in 1956. Given its size, it had become a major burden on the resources of the dwindling band of members. The building was named *Centenary House* and became the Hitchin Registrar's Office. After the sale, Friends met temporarily in the Lucas Room in the Town Hall.

[15]   Joshua Whiting's diary was published by Sarah Graham in 2006 – see page 101 for details

A new, more modest, building was proposed, the estimated cost with furnishings was £10,000. £6500 was to hand, including the proceeds from the sale of the 2nd building. A successful appeal was launched to raise the £3500 shortfall and the new building was constructed in the late 1950s. It is mounted on stilts over the Burial Ground and can be considered to be a very sensible and pragmatic solution in the prevailing circumstances. Some headstones were necessarily displaced and a few of the older families were against the change. The building won a Civic Trust Award in 1959.

TIME FOR CHANGE?

The strictures of the earliest principles had been increasingly challenged by the younger generations, particularly in the first half of the 19th century when the movement was perceived to be one where *"Everything is Nay never Yea"*. In a lengthy entry in his diary for 11th mo 30th 1838, William Lucas VI questions several of the long held views of the Society, in particular the denial of the use of the *heathen* names for days and months, saying: *"As to the names of days, months and so forth it is evident to me that our ancestors, who were but men in their zeal, carried their scruples to the borders of the ridiculous"*. In the following year he reports being admonished by John Whiting. *"Our honest friend J.W. has lately intimated to me that I cannot be made useful in the Society on account of unfaithfulness in these minor concerns such as dating a letter February."* Despite his misgivings, William was not one of those who left the Society and remained a committed and active member until his death in 1861.

A Quaker emphasis on plainness of living extended to clothing and entertainment. Simple clothes were required and the standard outside dress for women included *coal-scuttle* hats, as seen in the drawing on page 6, but according to Hine, *"young Quakeresses could wear them in such a way as to look positively becoming."* Quakers could always be identified by their style of dress but in 1845 an Epistle was issued by the Yearly Meeting warning against *"Those progressive deviations from simplicity of dress and that gradual assimilation with the world..."*, but the world was indeed changing and by 1860 the requirement for plainness of apparel had been abandoned.

Many popular pastimes were disallowed and Quakers consequently were great readers. Other indoor entertainments were restricted mostly to parlour and board games such as chess. Public shows, including circuses and fairs were strictly taboo. Matilda Lucas tells us that, as children, they were prohibited from visiting the circus in Butts Close and had to be content with watching the procession from the balcony of John Thompson's house in High Street. Musical instruments were frowned upon but here again, dissent was emerging, albeit in a very restrained manner.

In *A History of Hitchin*, Hine recounts the story of "The Piano", as told to him by Alice Moule, a daughter of Oswald Foster (Jnr). She recalls how she was taken on tiptoe to the top of the house of Joseph, Phebe's brother, by one of the younger generation and there secretly shown the first piano of the Hitchin Friends, and allowed to listen for a brief while to its *"unholy"* music. 'Old Joe', as he was called, was said to have never known of its existence. Matilda Lucas confirmed the story, saying that she was one of the first to know of the secret. This would have been in the 1850s/1860s. The house was probably Joseph's later one at Oakfield, St Ippollittes. [16] It is intriguing to find that after his death in 1877, the sale particulars of his effects at Oakfield list a *"fine-toned 7-octave Trichord Pianoforte, in Rosewood case by Collard & Collard"*. We don't know if Joseph finally gave his approval for the piano to be in his house, but surely he didn't remain oblivious to its existence for all of those years!

Hitchin Quakers at chess — From a Samuel Lucas drawing in Hitchin Museum.

DECLINE AND CONSOLIDATION

The construction of the second Meeting House in 1839 was indeed an *act of faith* as it was built at a time of considerable reduction in the membership. Not long before it was built, William Lucas V recorded in his diary on 12th mo 28th 1836 *"This year is remarkable for the great secession of members from our Society — owing to a considerable difference in religious views from those which had always been deemed our peculiar principles."* This was not just a local decline for on the 5th mo 23rd 1849 his son, William VI, wrote *"Yearly Meeting began: I never saw so small an attendance; we miss many of our standard bearers."*

Notwithstanding the opening of the new Meeting House, the drift from the Hitchin Meeting continued. In the 100 year period from 1750 to 1850, the membership halved from 200 to 100. This was despite amalgamations with other Meetings which had fared even more badly. The one surviving Friend at Baldock sent a plaintive plea to Hitchin Friends, begging them to come and sit with him. One of the main reasons for loss of members was the ban on marrying non-Quakers. The requirement to marry within the sect sprang from the earliest days of the movement but resulted in a large loss of members in the first half of the 19th century. Often, those that did remain found that there was a dearth of suitable partners and stayed unmarried as a result. The *marry within* requirement was annulled in 1859.

The decline continued over the next century. By 1940, the Hitchin membership had dropped to just a dozen or so and in 1973, Walter Lucas, a descendant of William Lucas VI, wrote that there was just one surviving Quaker in his branch of the family. However, Metford Robson reported in 2002 that the Meeting had settled to a healthy level of members and attracted a good number of young

---

[16] Various spellings of the name Ippollittes have been used over the years, but that favoured by Phebe has been used throughout this publication.

families, who are not necessarily members, but who enjoy their association with the Meeting.

EDUCATION AND BUSINESS

Quakers precluded themselves from professions where taking an oath was a condition of entry, so they turned their talents to the world of industry, banking and commerce, with some considerable success. The key to business success was education and a network of schools was established for Quaker children, both boys and girls. Some were truly Dickensian, in the worst sense of the word, but others, such as Ackworth [17], were (and are) centres of educational excellence. Ackworth was established by the London Meeting in 1779 and accepted girls from the outset. Phebe's mother, Hannah, was an early pupil (no. 445), attending the school from 1782, when she was eleven, to 1786, before moving to Esther Tuke's school for girls at York. Over one hundred years later, we find that Phebe's grandson, Arthur Reginald Glaisyer, attended Ackworth between 1891 and 1894, a very long way from his parental home in Clay County, Minnesota!

In business, Quakers believed that relations founded upon honesty and trust were an important factor in long term success. Personal profit, to the exclusion of the interests of others was unacceptable to most Quakers and they detested exploitation. Inevitably there were some notable exceptions, with two relations of Phebe: Isaac Bass (see page 72) and John Rickman (page 87), both of Sussex, being particular examples. In the latter part of the 19th century, the directors of the Quaker founded Bryant & May Match Company also lost sight of these high ideals, leading to the infamous East-London match-girls' strike of 1888. It is also true to say that Quakers were business opportunists. John Gray, the father-in-law of William Lucas III, is said to have made his fortune by giving away bibles to the unfortunates who were condemned to hang at Tyburn and at the same time selling them gin for whatever price they would pay for it!

Some nationally important businesses founded by Quakers include confectioners Cadbury, Fry and Rowntree; Clarks Shoes; Wedgwood china; Abraham Darby, Ironmaster at Coalbrookdale foundary; Huntley and Palmer biscuits; the Stockton & Darlington Railway; Barclays Bank – the list goes on. Inevitably, most of those that survive have passed into non-Quaker hands.

SOCIAL REFORM AND RELIEF WORK

With an abhorrence of injustice, many Quakers were philanthropists and were proactive in the fields of women's emancipation, equality of rights, the peace-movement, education for all and the abolition of capital punishment, invariably being far ahead of the prevailing attitudes of society in these matters.

Somewhat paradoxically, at the very time that the movement saw such a sharp decline in membership early in the 19th century, some of the most important

[17] Ackworth School near Pontefract was founded by John Fothergill in 1779 and became an important boarding school for Quaker boys and girls but it cannot be considered as fully co-educational, the sexes being taught separately in most classes. The school survives with a Quaker ethos but is now open to all, mostly day pupils.

social reform work was done by Quakers, especially in the fields of abolition of slavery and prison reform. Hitchin Friends were particularly active in the anti-slavery movement and we read that Phebe 'did her bit' by using honey as a sweetener as opposed to the sugar which was obtained by the labour of slaves (page 49). Samuel and William Lucas VI were good friends of Elizabeth Fry, the prison reformer.

Very much later, Quakers participated in the Kindertransport, where 10,000 Jewish children were evacuated from Europe during 1938-1939. Other opportunities for humanitarian work in Hitler's Europe were understandably limited, but Quakers carried out war relief work wherever they could. That work was recognised in 1947 when the Quaker movement, represented by the Friends' Service Council [18] in London and the American Friends' Service Committee[19], was awarded the Nobel Peace Prize. The citation stating that:

"The Quakers have shown us that it is possible to translate into action what lies deep in the hearts of many: compassion for others and the desire to help them — that rich expression of the sympathy between all men, regardless of nationality or race, which, transformed into deeds, must form the basis for lasting peace. For this reason alone the Quakers deserve to receive the Nobel Peace Prize today."

These ideals have been pursued to the current day and Quakers remain involved in peace, humanitarian and relief work throughout the world.

The third (and current) Hitchin Friends' Meeting House at No 1 Payne's Park, Hitchin. Photographed by the author in April 2009.

---

[18] Originally the Friends' Foreign Mission Association, formed in 1868, it has now evolved into the Quaker Peace & Social Witness.

[19] The American Friends' Service Committee was founded in 1917 to provide conscientious objectors an opportunity to serve those in need, instead of fighting. The organisation survives to the current day.

Chapter 3

The Lucas Brewery

The Early Years

The early origins of the Lucas involvement in brewing are somewhat shrouded in the mists of time. In *Brewers in Hertfordshire*, Allan Whitaker [20] records that William Lucas (II) started brewing in 1709 at an unknown Hitchin location. Moving into brewing was a natural business expansion for the Lucas's as they already owned several maltings [21] around the town.

In addition to brewing, William Lucas II was a draper & woolstapler (a dealer in wool), but seemingly also indulged in banking activities as he held a mortgage on the Angel Street/Sun Street brewing and malting premises occupied by John and Ann Draper and William and Elizabeth Conquest. In 1736 he obtained complete ownership of the property, which had been in use by the Draper family for brewing and malting from at least as far back as 1676.

In his will, proved in 1748, William Lucas II left the brewery estate to his eldest son William III, but unfortunately that son died only 3 years after his father, leaving a widow, Phebe (née Gray), and three children. The business was then managed in the form of a trust by her uncle, the highly respected Isaac Gray, who is also believed to have invested a large capital sum into it and traded under the name of Gray & Lucas. On coming of age in 1765, William Lucas IV inherited his share of the brewery and continued in partnership with Isaac.

The 1773 marriage deed of settlement of William IV upon his second wife, Susanna Camps, contains the following description of the brewery property:

---

[20] Brewers in Hertfordshire, page 138.

[21] Malting is a process applied to cereal grains, in which the grains are made to germinate by soaking in water and then quickly halted from further germinating by drying/heating with hot air. This process converts the grain starches into the sugars needed for the brewing process.

Samuel Spavold (1708-1795) Attriuted to Samuel Lucas. Reproduced from The History of Hitchin.

"All that capital messuage[22] *or Tenement with the appurtenances in Hitchin in a certain street there called Angel Street, otherwise Saint Mary's-street, heretofore in the occupation of Edward Draper, gentleman, deceased, and also all of those barns, houses, outhouses, edifices, and all that yard with the appurtenances situate lying and being towards the south part of the said Capital Messuage or Tenement, late also in the occupation of the said Edward Draper, heretofore purchased of Daniel Spencer, gentleman, and George Audley, with the Malthouse Brewhouse and other Houses there erected, and also all those five cottages or Tenements with the appurtenances situate in a street called Bridge-street in Hitchin aforesaid, near the River there and adjoining to the said capital messuage or the yard and outhouses thereof, and four of which have been converted into Storehouses and the other is now in the occupation of Samuel Spavold".*[23]

Samuel Spavold appears to have been in trouble with the Court Leet[24] in 1778 as the records show the following entry: *"...an Incroachment has been made upon the soil and land of the Lord of this Manor by Samuel Spavold, who hath inclosed and built upon and converted to his own Use the Bank and part of the Soil of the River near his Dwelling House in the town of Hitchin within the said Manor".*

The decision of the court is unknown but it certainly didn't result in the removal of the *"Incroachment"*. In a letter to a local newspaper in 1923, C. Loftus Barham wrote *"The above property* [The Brewery] *is now possibly changing hands, and it might be a good opportunity for the Urban Council to ... effect the removal of a building which causes a nuisance to the neighbourhood, besides being an unauthorised encroachment on the river".*

The building is visible on the very left hand side of the Madge Thompson's watercolour shown on the cover of this book. It was finally removed in the 1960s but the ground on which it stood can still be seen from the Hiz Bridge, still encroaching into the river!

---

[22] A messuage equates to a dwelling-house and includes outbuildings, orchard, curtilage or court-yard and garden. A capital messuage is the main messuage of an estate, the house in which the owner of the estate normally lives.

[23] Samuel Spavold married Phebe Gray in 1766, 15 years after the death of her first husband, William Lucas III. Samuel was a master carpenter but devoted most of his later life to the Society of Friends. He became a travelling minister of international repute, visiting Friends in much of Britain, Ireland and North America, but according to Hine, his sermons were "dry and tedious". They were also over-long and at some meetings the congregation quietly drifted away, seemingly unbeknown to him as he held forth.

[24] Court Leet – Manorial courts which dealt with petty law and order and the administration of communal agriculture. Courts Leet have now been superseded by magistrates courts.

Isaac Gray was a Quaker travelling minister and died in Ireland in 1784. Upon his death, the brewery reverted to full Lucas ownership and William V was indentured in that same year[25]. William Lucas IV retired from business in 1796 leaving its management in the hands of his sons William V and Joseph (Snr — Phebe's father)

The brewery site was substantially rebuilt in 1771 and the leading on one of the buildings displayed that date until it was demolished in the early 1960s. The Brewery House in Sun Street was rebuilt in the early 1780s and became the family home for several generations of Lucas. William Lucas IV occupied it in its earliest days but he moved to Western House in Tilehouse Street when he withdrew from the brewery affairs. Phebe's father, Joseph, then became the householder. He took his new bride, Hannah, to the house in 1798 and their children, including Phebe, were all to be born there. [26]

Samuel Spavold's 'Incroachment' into the Hiz still survives beside the new apartments which have been built on the brewery site. Photographed by the author in April 2009.

19ᵀᴴ CENTURY EVENTS

Brief glimpses of events at the brewery are contained in the diary of William Lucas V:

7th mo 21st 1817 — *"Began to pull down part of our Brewhouse & kiln house loft & Brewhouse storehouse – in order to erect a new copper in a different situation, & make a tun room."*[27]

5th mo 30th 1831 — *"Put up a refrigerator to cool down worts".*

1st mo 2nd 1832 — *"Last night or early this morning our new counting house & yeast room broken into by thieves and abt. £5 or £6 stolen, & a great coat."*

2nd mo 24th 1836 — *"Very great alterations are going on at the Brewhouse dwelling house which now exhibits a scene of desolation."*

Phebe recalls that the Brewery House was subject to regular flooding (page 57) and William Lucas V confirms this in his diary. In an entry for 4th mo 12th 1823, he records *"Much rain last night and nearly the whole day – at one time*

[25] The indenture document survives in Hitchin Museum, showing that William V was to be "an apprentice in the arts of a brewer and maltster".

[26] The Brewery House is allegedly the most haunted in Hitchin. The Lucas family are said to have subdued a ghost called Elizabeth by saying "Goodnight Elizabeth, Pax Vobiscum" (Peace be with you). No reference to the haunting has been found in any of the Lucas papers researched.

[27] In brewing, a tun was a fermenting vat.

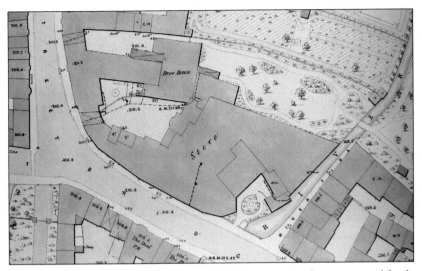

An extract from the 1851 Ordnance Survey ten foot to one mile scale map, prepared for the local Board of Health, showing the Lucas brewery property in Sun Street & Bridge Street, Hitchin. Hitchin Museum

threatening to flood the Dwelling house at Brew-house". Again, on 5th mo 24th 1831 whilst in London, he wrote "*We were informed that at Hitchin a violent storm of thunder & lightening occurred at 8 o clock in ye morning which flooded in some degree the lower rooms of the Brewhouse.*" The flooding caused by water from heavy rain rushing down Tilehouse Street was to be a continuing problem until well into the 20th century.

William Lucas V also mentions some of the brewery workers but, unfortunately, mostly upon their demise! His diary entries include:

6th mo 21st 1805 — "*Wm Sexton, our brewer was buried today. He having been a Volunteer* [[28]], *a number of ye Corps attended and performed what is termed, military honours. He had been ill upwards of ten weeks with dropsy* [[29]] *& died aged 29 on the 19th".*

10th mo 16th 1810 — "*This day our foreman John Dunnage died*"

2nd mo 12th 1831 — "*Feelings dull at parting this afternoon with my respected friend Thomas Marsh who for 18 years has been our clerk & who has now engaged with Thomas Burr, Brewer, Dunstable".*

---

[28] The Hitchin Loyal Volunteer Association was formed in c.1798 over fears of an uprising of the "lower classes" similar to the revolution in France, but it was disbanded in 1802. When the war with France recommenced in 1803, the government called for the Volunteer Corps to be reformed, and the ex-members of the Loyal Volunteer Association would have been the first to answer the call. A vellum roll of the Volunteer Corps is to be found in Hitchin Museum.

[29] Dropsy is an abnormal accumulation of fluid beneath the skin. In this day and age it is more likely to be called an oedema.

4th mo 22nd 1831 — *"Died George Westwood aged 53 he was our brewer and had lived with us near 29 years".*

6th mo 2nd 1831 — *"Died Wm. Child, Brewer & Cooper, after 2 days seizure with a brain fever, aged abt. 33".*

3rd mo 2nd 1832 — *"We heard that William Law formerly our malt maker, & who of late has lived in London, has died of Cholera Morbus."*

10th mo 28th 1833 —*"George Osborn worker died of Cholera"*

7th mo 25th 1836 — *"Died our malt maker William Cook aged 67"*

William VI barely mentions the brewery in his diaries but, not one to *suffer fools gladly,* he does refer to Thomas Marsh in a somewhat disparaging manner. In describing a nearly missed rendezvous at Charing Cross in London, when returning to Hitchin from school at Bristol, he writes: *"…I found our clerk, Thomas Marsh, not the most acute of mortals…"* We shall probably never know what caused Thomas to depart from the brewery after eighteen years of service, but the prospect of working for the younger William, who would have been by then taking an increasingly important role in its management and who obviously had little regard for Thomas, may have been a significant factor.

William V retired from the Brewery in 1839 and as Joseph (Snr) had died in 1832, responsibility for its management was passed to William VI and Joseph (Jnr – Phebe's brother). Samuel (the artist) was also a working partner in the

Coopers busy in the brewery yard, taken in the early 20th century. Hitchin Museum

firm from 1834, but was 'indulged' by his brother William to allow him time to also pursue his artistic interests.

In addition to malting and brewing, the business expanded to include tied houses in Hitchin and further afield in North Hertfordshire and Bedfordshire. In 1834 there were thirty houses owned directly by the brewery and eleven others owned by various members of the family. The brewery site was gradually developed to provide additional facilities including cooperage and mineral water production.

Phebe describes the brewery gardens in her recollections and Matilda Lucas provides additional information. In her memories of Hitchin, told to Reginald Hine in 1930, she says: *"Quakers were great garden grabbers, adding to their own those which should have belonged to other houses. The Brewery garden went up to the Swimming Bath and then right away to Queen Street. Through a malting, you could get into Bridge Street. There was no limit to the fruit grown and eaten by us in that garden".* The River Hiz runs along the south-east boundary of the brewery site. The flow was reported to be very seasonal, prompting Francis Lucas to write *"in the winter we refer to the river as the 'IZ, and in the summer, when it dries up, as the WAS",* but according to Matilda Lucas, the river never did run dry.

TEMPERANCE ANGST

The essential principles of the Quaker movement, established in the earliest days, did not impose abstinence but in Victorian times the Quaker temperance voice became increasingly important and several members of the Lucas family were known to have become ambivalent about their involvement with the brewing trade. Joseph Lucas (Jnr) and Williams V and VI were all known to have had misgivings about the business. Other Quakers were very proactive in the Temperance movement. Samuel Bowly, a nephew of Ann (Bowly) Lucas, gave lectures at the Town Hall. Matilda Lucas recalls that a woman had two glasses of beer before a meeting in case she could never have any afterwards. Bowly was a powerful speaker and a 3-bottle man in the audience of one meeting is reported to have knocked off two of them!

Although he barely mentions the brewery in his diaries, William VI did agonise over being involved in the trade. In an entry in his diary for 3rd mo 17th 1839, he wrote *"There are no doubt objections to our business and many things in it very unpleasant, but still as far as I can at present see, my duty is to continue in it, and endeavour to conduct it as respectably as possible".* It is evident that the question of abstinence was a matter of great debate among Friends of the day as two years later, on 4th mo 8th 1841, he wrote *"I often feel misgivings as to the propriety of holding Public House property that I wish we were fairly out of the business; but then again it seems necessary to provide for the settlement of my six sons."* Also *"John Whiting,* [30] *who is a great advocate, and support of teetotalism in Hitchin, has been frequently obliged by the doctor's order's to resume Beer, and to-day we hear that he is again ill. Total abstinence is certainly irrational, unchristian and inexpedient, temperance is quite another thing."* He also expressed the wish that none of his

---

[30]   A leading member of the Hitchin Meeting.

sons would enter the business, but this was not to be, as William VII became a partner and remained as such until his retirement in 1894, although all of the others did manage to 'escape' into other professions.

Joseph (Jnr) appears to have dissociated himself from brewery affairs by 1861, as in the census for that year he is shown as living at Oakfield House at St Ippollittes (now Kingshott School) and describes himself as a *landed proprietor*, rather than as a *common brewer*, which occupation he had declared in the census ten years previously. None of his sons entered the brewery; indeed, they all left Hitchin to pursue their careers elsewhere. Joseph did, however, retain some interest in the licensed trade until the time of his death, as the final sale of his assets included seventeen licensed premises, all of which had been leased to the Lucas brewery. The sale, in July 1883, resulted in nine of these being purchased by Samuel Lucas.

BREWERY HOUSE OCCUPANTS AND SOME LONG-SERVING EMPLOYEES

After Joseph's move to Oakfield House, the Brewery House appears to have remained empty for a number of years, being shown as unoccupied in the 1861 and 1871 census. Its status is unclear in 1881 but in 1891 was occupied by William Arnold (a tailor) and his family. In 1901 it was occupied by George Taylor, who was recorded as a brewer's clerk with his son, also George, being a brewer's secretary. The Taylor family were still resident in the Brewery House in 1911, but by then George senior was brewery manager and his son was the clerk. A 1917 article in the *Pictorial Record* recorded that George Taylor had been associated

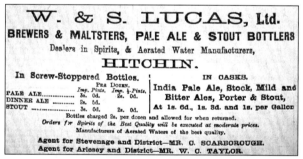

A 1904 advertisement for the Lucas Brewery from the Hertfordshire Express. Of the two agents, Christopher Scarborough was a shopkeeper living with his family at Holmsdale Terrace, Stevenage. W. C. Taylor has not been identified.
Lawson Thompson Scrapbook, Hitchin Museum

with the brewery for 32 years, but he had retired by 1919.

Another family with a long association with the brewery were the Jeeves, with two generations being employed from at least 1841 until 1898. They lived in the Brewer's House which was within the brewery grounds and had the address of No.1 Bridge Street (see the photograph on page 38). In 1841, John Jeeves was recorded as a brewer but by 1851 had become a brewer's clerk. He died in 1861 and his son, also John, then became the clerk and retained that position until his death in 1898. His widow, Emma, was still resident at the house in 1911. She died in 1919.

SALE OF THE BREWERY AND FINAL CLOSURE

The brewery became a limited company in 1898 but the end was in sight. In 1906, just three years before its bicentenary, William Lucas VII wrote an embittered letter to *The Standard*, entitled *"The Burden of the Middle-Class"* bemoaning the heavy taxation and duties imposed on the brewing trade, claiming that it was being *"taxed out of existence to support a huge force of Bumbledom and officialism larger than any standing army in Europe"*.

The catalyst for the final disposal was the death of Samuel Lucas (Jnr), in 1919, as by that time he and his son Stephen were the surviving working partners. Samuel had been very dynamic in the brewing industry with interests in the North American trade and also in the north of England. He is said to have crossed the Atlantic 36 times. After his death, there doesn't appear to have been any appetite, or capacity, within the family to continue the business. It was advertised for sale in 1921 and purchased by J. W. Green of Luton [31] on 29th June 1923, six Lucas family members being signatories to the conveyance. A local newspaper announcement of the sale stated that the Lucas operation would be retained as a distinct branch of the Luton company but, just a few months later, it had been completely closed.

---

[31]   J.W. Green was subsequently renamed Flowers and was later absorbed into the Whitbread empire. The Luton site closed in 1968.

HITCHIN BREWERY.

ACQUIRED BY MESSRS. J. W. GREEN LIMITED.

Mesrs. J. W. Green, Ltd., of The Luton Brewery, have acquired the old established Hitchin Brewery of Messrs. W. S. Lucas, Ltd. It is not an amalgamation of interests such as generally appear to be the order of the day, but it is an acquisition by Messrs. J. W. Green, Ltd., and, we understand, will be conducted entirely distinct from the business of The Luton Brewery.

The Hitchin Brewery was established in 1750 and the business includes some 50 licensed houses in Herts and Beds. It is not proposed even to alter the name of the concern; the whole of the original shares have been purchased by Messrs. Green, Ltd., and the new Board of Directors numbers three, namely :—Mr. S. J. Green, J.P. (Chairman), Lieut-Colonel H. P. Green, and Mr. W. W. Merchant.

Samuel Lucas (Jnr) in 1905 – his death in 1919 was the catalyst which led to the sale of the brewery.
From the Lawson Thompson scrapbook in Hitchin Museum.

A newspaper cutting reporting the sale of the Lucas Brewery in 1923.
Lawson Thompson Scrapbook, Hitchin Museum

The sale to Greens had included 51 tied houses; this was in addition to another 40 houses which the family had previously sold. It is not hard to draw the conclusion that the acquisition by Greens was just to lay hands on the Lucas assets, in particular the tied houses, given that the Lucas Brewery was closed with almost indecent haste, although the economic climate and problems of water supply were the published reasons for closure. Much of the equipment was moved to Luton. The closure would have adversely affected a number of families. In the 1881 census, William Lucas VII recorded that 32 men were employed. This had dropped to about 25 at the time of the closure, still a substantial number for a non-industrial town such as Hitchin.

A newspaper report shows that Greens disposed of the site by auction on 29th July 1924 for a total of £2,275, the purchaser being Mr Hugh Smyth. The sale particulars described the site thus: *"Comprising the freehold business premises, lately forming a portion of the Hitchin Brewery, with frontage to Bridge-street, and substantially built warehouses with a covered floor space of over 5,300 feet super, together with the residence used as the brewer's house and large garden with lawn. The total area being about 17,500 feet super"*. It is interesting to note that Lucas owned houses, no's 6 to 10 Tilehouse Street, were sold in the same auction by W & S Lucas Ltd to Mr R Saunders, for a total of £1,225.

From Closure to the Present Day

After closure, the brewery site had various uses, part of it being used as the Sales motor garage until the 1960s. In c1920s some of the brewery buildings on the corner of Sun Street and Bridge Street, were replaced by the building now occupied by Acorn Estate Agents and the Graham Ranger Beauty Salon. The building initially became office accommodation, occupied by Hertfordshire County Council and the Ministry of Works. The remaining brewery buildings were demolished in 1963 to make way for the very much unloved utilitarian Crown House tax office. That in turn was demolished in 2006/2007 and the site is now occupied by apartments, although Phebe's Brewery House still survives and for the last 72 years has been the premises of Philpotts of Hitchin, Furnishers.

Chapter 4

Two Further Hitchin Locations

Two further Hitchin locations are particularly important in Phebe's narrative – West Mill and the property in Cock Street.

WEST MILL

As the crow flies, West Mill [32] lies just over a mile and a quarter to the north-west of Hitchin Market Place. It stands on the River Oughton (spelt Orton in older times), which rises at Oughtonhead. The river is very short, flowing for just two miles before its confluence with the Hiz at Ickleford. The River Oughton and West Mill were once a detached area of Bedfordshire, surrounded by Hertfordshire, so one finds that the address of the mill was given as West Mill, Shillington, Beds. An Act of 1844 transferred the river and mill into Hertfordshire and at the same time resolved many other such anomalies throughout the country.

Opinions differ regarding the origins of the mill. In an article in *Hertfordshire Countryside* magazine [33], Cyril Moore reports that it was constructed by Richard Lucas, miller of Walsworth (he is shown in *The Descent of the Lucas Family* on page 90), towards the end of the sixteenth century and that his son Edward, of Alton Mill, built a house beside West Mill and lived in it. Edward died in June 1650 so *"the house must date from early in the seventeenth century"*. However, H G Western in *A History of Ickleford* (1975) considered that West Mill was probably a mill referred to in 1317 as Lewins. Thomas Ansell became Lord of the Manor of Ickleford in 1587. On his death in 1606 he left the manor to his eldest son, Thomas, but West Mill was left to one of his younger sons, Edward Ansell (*A History of Ickleford* p.9). Also, the Hitchin manor court book for 23 October 1695 has a reference to John Papworth alias Bradwell who occupied West Mill near the manor of Hitchin.

In 1807, Phebe's Uncle Samuel and Aunt Phebe Allen became the tenants of the mill, upon the death of the previous tenant, James Whittingstall, and remained there until the lease expired in 1829. Phebe's recollection of her visits

---

[32] Often spelt 'Westmill' these days but the form favoured by Phebe is used throughout this publication.

[33] Hertfordshire Countryside magazine, April 1967 edition, page 738.

West Mill in 1904   Lawson Thompson Scrapbook — Hitchin Museum.

there would have thus been during the 1820s. Her cousin William Lucas VI also recorded holidays spent with the Allens. He writes *"Our half-holidays were often spent at West Mill where our Uncle and Aunt Allen then resided; punting on the river in the old flat-bottom boat, donkey riding, bathing, cricketing, bat folding* [34], *were our amusements."*. He also recorded that West Mill was cut off for *"some weeks"* in the severe winter of 1813-1814 *"by the deep snow which quite filled up the road from the top of the hedge on one side to the other"* and that his father mounted a rescue mission for the residents of the mill.

William Lucas V wrote in 1839 *"A melancholy circumstance occurred this morning. The wife of William Bowyer wandered out early from her bed & threw herself into the River at West Mill & was taken out lifeless"*. She is said to still haunt the area. In 1841 the occupant is recorded as William Cox.

By 1867, water flow was a serious issue as George Beaver, the Hitchin Surveyor, was requested to check levels at the mill to assess the feasibility of reducing the river bed to aid the flow. Whether or not this took place is unclear but milling continued into the 20th century and the 1901 census shows Ernest Bowman listed as resident at West Mill House, with his family, his occupation being a flour miller. Milling activities at West Mill finally succumbed to adverse economic conditions in the 1920s. The mill was severely damaged by fire in 1961 and Ordnance Survey maps of the period show it to be disused. The buildings have now been converted into desirable residences.

---

[34] Very possibly refers to making and flying paper 'bats', bearing in mind that he was writing well before the days of aeroplanes.

THE COCK STREET/HIGH STREET PROPERTY

The Lucas family had a long association with the site which now consists of numbers 9, 10 and 11 High Street, and which stands between the Cock public house and the Natwest Bank. In earlier times, High Street was called Cock Street, the name being changed in the 1850s. William Lucas I owned a shop, malting and barns at the site. Until the first Hitchin Quaker Meeting House was completed in 1694, the early meetings were held at the Lucas house.

The property was still in full Lucas ownership in 1748 but their malting operations were transferred to other locations and by 1818, number 10 had become the premises of the Jermyn draper shop and was later the premises of the Perks & Llewellyn chemist and lavender business. In 1961, the Perks shop, then owned by Miss V. Lewis, was demolished and replaced by the ex-Woolworths building. The historical interior of the chemists shop is now installed at Hitchin Museum

An extract from the 1851 Ordnance Survey large scale map of Hitchin, showing the Thompson property at number 11 Cock Street (now High Street). West Lane (now Payne's Park) is on the left and Cock Street on the right. The single storey buildings referred to by Matilda Lucas can be seen at the lower boundary of the property and are possibly disused maltings. The stables and coach-house can be seen centre left, with access from West Lane. The summerhouse referred to by both Phebe and Matilda is near the bottom left corner of the map-extract. The vegetation depiction is symbolised so it is not possible to identify the exact position of the mulberry tree which is referred to by both Phebe and Matilda and which, according to Phebe, was still fruiting in 1890. — Hitchin Museum

Of more relevance to Phebe's story is the property, now number 11 and occupied by Café Rouge, the Optometrist opticians and the aptly named Regent Cottage Chinese Restaurant. We are told by Phebe that in the early 19th century, a shop here was occupied by Atkins, a butcher, probably on lease, but the gardens behind were still used by the Lucas family. William Lucas V recorded that Atkins died on 6th mo 24th 1831 and this provided an opportunity to redevelop number 11.

In the 1820s, John Thompson had become the proprietor of the Jermyn draper shop at number 10. In 1830, he married Mary, the daughter of William Lucas V. Upon Atkins' demise, a new shop, with living accommodation above, was constructed for the Thompsons by William. In a diary entry for 4th mo 1st 1833 William V records *"Began to pull down in order to rebuild ye Cock Street House"*.

Construction took just less than a year as two diary entries in 1834 record:

HITTCHIN,_____ 1876.

Mr. John Randall

To JOHN THOMPSON & SON, Dr.,

Linen and Woollen Drapers, Hatters, Clothiers, &c.

Jany 11	Overcoat for William	2	7	6
May 27	Suit for Charles	3	5	
Aug 26	M Trousers	1		
Nov 16	Boys Suit	1	1	
		7	13	6

An 1877 receipt from John Thompson's draper shop to W. John Randall, demonstrating a charming informality: "Overcoat for William" and "Suit for Charles". Unfortunately, I have been unable find any further information about the Randall family.

An early 20th C. view of the Thompson draper and tailor shop at No. 11 High Street. The balcony mentioned by Matilda Lucas can be seen. The two assistants standing at the front of the shop are William Pearce (right) and William Belstead. Pearce was born in Salisbury but had a long association with the Thompsons in Hitchin as he is shown residing at the premises in the 1881, 1891 and 1901 census. William Belstead was born in Hitchin and lived in Grammar School Walk. In the 1901 census, his mother Ann is shown as being the caretaker of the Friends' Meeting House. From a photograph in the Lawson Thompson scrapbook in Hitchin Museum.

1st mo 24th 1834 *"This evenng a supper was provided of which abt. 90 partook on account of ye nearly finished state of J Thompson's house in Cock Street the company for ye most part consisting of those who had any hand in ye undertaking."* And in the 3rd mo 1834 *"About ye 10th of this month my son and daughter Thompson were able to move into their new house to reside, ye trade having been moved thereto several days before."*

The ex-Thompson building in High Street, Hitchin, built for John and Mary Thompson by William Lucas V in 1834. Photographed in April 2009 by the author.

In addition to the description of the garden provided by Phebe, Matilda Lucas provides more information about the Thompsons and their property. She records that it was poorly ventilated and became very insanitary. Lawson (son of John and Mary) contracted typhoid fever and the drains were consequently overhauled.

Matilda recalled that the Thompson and Lucas children were not allowed to visit the circuses held at Butts Close, but were permitted to view processions and other street performances from the balcony which once adorned the front of the Thompson house.

A first-floor front room contained John Thompson's renowned library. For 50 years it was also the depository of the British & Foreign Bible Society. His personal library included much material relating to The Society of Friends and also many other historically important volumes.

The library attracted many visitors to the house, including Lord Lytton and Matthew Arnold, the poet son of Thomas Arnold of Rugby School fame. Matilda also describes *"At right angles to the main part of the house ran a long row of buildings one storey high, rooms and offices opening out of each other beginning with the study above and the kitchen below. I do not know if they were older buildings; they ended in a little yard with a stable and coach-house."* These buildings are visible on the 1851 Ordnance Survey map of Hitchin and are thought to be the Maltings referred to by Phebe. All have long since been demolished.

Of the garden Matilda wrote *"Like many Quaker gardens, it enclosed what should have belonged to other houses and one side of Brand Street had to put up with back yards. The garden widened out at the top"* ... *"in one corner was an old thatched summer house, and there was a mulberry tree on the grass plot. When the fruit was ripe, children used to call in the most shameless manner."*

The drapery and tailoring business became a surprisingly large employer and by the time of the 1871 census, John Thompson records that he was employing 16 men and 5 boys. John died in 1877 and Lawson then became the proprietor of the business. By 1901, the three surviving Thompson siblings — Lawson, Margaret and Mary, none of whom had married – had moved to a new house at Elmside in Bedford Road, which Hine later described in Hitchin Worthies: *"Elmside! The gathering place of wit, hospitality, and human kindness. The happy resort of men-of-letters, of artists, of divines. The spring and centre of quiet, unassuming work of the well-being and happiness of others. The home of three people whose like for singularity of charm and natural goodness will never be seen again."*

In the 1881 census, Phebe is shown as visiting Lawson. No other reference to Phebe visiting Hitchin after her marriage in 1844 has been found.

Lawson continued in business in the High Street shop until 1902 when he retired at the age of 65. He was still very active in local affairs and became chairman of Hitchin Urban District Council in 1903.

Hitchin Museum records show that the High Street premises were sold by auction in 1906, but continued in use as a tailoring establishment until 1986, latterly as part of the Hepworth's chain. The ground floor has been the premises of Café Rouge for the last ten years or so.

Chapter 5

Recollection of My Childhood

by Phebe Glaisyer

The following pages contain a transcription of the actual narrative as set down by Phebe Glaisyer in 1890. She wrote unbroken continuous prose. For the purposes of this book, sub-titles and explanatory footnotes have been introduced.

At the end of her narrative, Phebe drew family trees of the wider family where known to her. These are shown at Appendix B as Family Trees 1 to 6 (pages 91 to 97).

Hitchin Museum in Payne's Park, the repository for Phebe's journal and many other original sources used herein. If not for the museum, this publication would not have been possible. Photographed in April 2009 by the author.

The Brewery House – Hitchin Museum
(Phebe attached a print of this photograph to the inside front cover of her manuscript notebook)

"**O**n the opposite page is a picture of the old family house at Hitchin attached to the Brewery, it was always known as "The Brewhouse" [35], where our ancestors had lived for many generations; and the early home of the writer of the following pages. Tradition says that Queen Anne once lodged in the house on one of her journeys."

ON the *Twenty sixth* - Day of the *eighth* · Month, One Thousand *eight* Hundred and *sixteen* - - - *was* born - - - *at Hitchin* · - - · - · · - · in the Parish - - - *of Hitchin* - - - - · · · · in the *County* of *Hertford* unto *Joseph Lucas* - - - · · · *Brewer* - · · · · and *Hannah* · his Wife, - - · *a Daughter* - · who · *is* · named *Phebe* - · - - · - · · · · - - - · -

We, who were present at the said Birth, have subscribed our Names as Witnesses thereof.

Oswald Foster
Ann Lucas
Phebe Allen

The Religious Society of Friends Bedfordshire and Hertfordshire Quarterly Meeting birth record for Phebe Lucas. The three witnesses to her birth were Oswald Foster (Surgeon) and her aunts Ann Lucas and Phebe Allen, all of whom are later mentioned in her text. Author's Collection.
It can be seen that she was indeed named "Phebe" as opposed to the more commonly used "Phoebe". The "Phebe" name variant was introduced into the Lucas family by Phebe Gray, (our) Phebe's great-grandmother.

---

[35] It is not totally clear if 'Brewhouse' refers to just the house or the whole brewery. In his diary, William Lucas V refers to the house as "The Dwelling house at the Brewhouse"

RECOLLECTIONS OF MY CHILDHOOD

I have very often of late called to mind the circumstances of my own childhood, how very differently was I situated from my dear grandchildren in this country, and those in their distant American home, and I wish for their sakes that I could depict somewhat of my home and surroundings in the early years of my life, as I think it may be interesting for my young descendants to know a little of their ancestors, some of whom probably they have as yet never heard of. The memory of them to myself is very precious and fresh, and I consider it an honour to have numbered among my near relations many who were of the excellent of the earth.

I was born at Hitchin a pleasant little country town in Hertfordshire on the 26th of 8th mo 1816, and was the youngest child of Joseph & Hannah Lucas. I have five brothers, Joseph, Edward, Charles, Thomas Woolston & Jeffrey, and one sister Sarah more than four years older than myself. My mother's maiden name was Hannah Woolston, she was an only child. She lost her parents when quite young and was brought up by her uncle Thomas Woolston who was a farmer at Irthlingborough Northamptonshire. I can just remember his venerable appearance when he came to our house to visit my parents.

My mother received her education first at Ackworth and afterwards at York School [36]. From some of her letters to my father before they were married (then in the possession of my brother Joseph) I find that she was inoculated for the small pox, and went to be under medical care during the time to a place appointed for patients, and passed safely through the complaint. It must have been a great change for her to become on her marriage the mistress of a rather large house to which the Brewery my uncle and father were engaged in was attached, also to join a pretty large circle of relations at Hitchin.

I greatly regret that I remember so little of her myself, but from the testimony of others I believe her to have been a sweet, gentle, woman and most exemplary in fulfilling her duties as a wife and mother. I have only a slight remembrance of her, but recall her as rather tall and slight with dark hair. I remember being with her sometimes when she changed her dress in the afternoon and thinking how nice she looked. I do not know much of the early life of my brothers, excepting brother Jeffery who was educated in Hitchin.

The master of the Free School, Dr. Niblock [37], was a well educated man who also had a private school of his own which my brother attended. I think my father was unwilling to part with him, he was a gentle and

[36] The first Quaker school for girls in York began in 1785 when Esther Tuke took girls into her house in Trinity Street. This is probably the school referred to by Phebe.

[37] See page 88 in the Biographical Details chapter for more on Joseph Niblock.

affectionate boy and endeared himself much to those he lived with. My eldest brother Joseph was living at home and was engaged in the malting business. Edward was serving his time with our cousin Isaac Bass at Brighton, [38] Charles was apprenticed to Glaisyer & Kemp [39] also at Brighton, Thomas was at Epping School, Jeffrey & Sarah were at home with myself, the youngest of the flock at the time these records begin. Sarah went to a day school kept by two worthy women, Mary & Ann Read, who taught reading, writing, a little arithmetic, and plain needlework, in which useful art their pupils excelled. She made shirts there for my father with beautiful stitching in them. I was never a pupil there, as the school was given up before I was old enough to go. My sister and I were not much of companions at that time, there was considerable difference in our age, her health was not strong and she was never fond of the outdoor games of children that I delighted in, her enjoyment was in reading. She began very early to store her mind with a great variety of useful and interesting literature in poetry as well as prose, so that as years advanced she became a most interesting and intellectual companion.

ILLNESS AND DEATH OF HER MOTHER

❙❙From my earliest recollections I believe that my dearest mother became a confirmed invalid. I do not think she was able to leave the house much, she sometimes went out for a drive in a pony chaise procured for her and driven mostly by my cousins Mary or Martha Lucas[40]. I was often allowed to accompany them. Our cousin Sarah Woolston was nearly always at our house to assist in the domestic management and care of my mother. As she became weaker I remember a nice resting couch being bought for her, different from the straight backed sofas then in use. She must have been in an advanced stage of her illness as I have a vague recollection of my dear father one evening carrying her from it up to her chamber, which I think she never left again. I was about 6½ years old when she died and well do I remember that I was at the house of my father's clerk Thomas Marsh who lived but a few steps from our premises. I suppose I was sent there to spend the morning with their daughter Eliza who was a constant play-fellow of mine. Our housemaid Sally Pack came to fetch me home, she was crying and we were then told that my dear mother had passed away [41]. Oh it is bitter enough even to [a] very young child to lose a tender mother. I found that the loss is indeed irreparable, there was a void that was never filled, and I shed many a tear in secret over the memory of the past young as I was, and recalled certain times when

---

[38]   Isaac Bass, a wealthy Brighton grocer and businessman – see Biographical Details, page 72.

[39]   Glaisyer & Kemp, Apothecaries- Phebe was to later marry into the Glaisyer family

[40]   Mary and Martha Lucas, the twin daughters of Ann (née Bowly) and William Lucas V. Mary later married John Thompson. Martha remained unmarried.

[41]   Hannah died on the 15th of the 3rd month 1823.

I had been disobedient to this precious mother with the keenest self reproach, and in the words of Jane Taylor's Hymn [42] could say from my own experience

"Oh if she would but come again
I think I'd vex her so no more"

From this time our cousin Sarah Woolston lived with us entirely as housekeeper. I have often thought since that she must have had an arduous post. Though she had the best intentions and wishes to fulfil her duty, she was not adapted to guide and restrain a lively and impetuous child as I then was and I am sure I was very disobedient and rebellious to her. She had not been used to children, and perhaps expected too much from me, and had no idea of winning me to do what she wished by meeting me half way as it were, so that any relations with her were not always of a pleasant kind to look back upon, tho' I do remember pleasant times with "cousin", as we called her, when she and I were together of a winters' evening in our handsome old wainscotted parlour, after learning my lessons for next day I would sometimes read a little to her, or would play games with the letters, and it was the practise to read one of the Olney Hymns [43] before going to bed.

THE BREWERY HOUSE IN SUN STREET

II may say that our dining room used to be much admired. It was a wainscoted room, and the panels of dark imitation of walnut wood were relieved by mouldings of maize colour. There were three windows in the room, two looking into the street and one into the yard, and as they all had window seats we liked to sit there and see what went on in the street. The back window gave us a view of the counting house where I have often seen my father and uncle sitting at their respective desks.

By daylight our parlour looked bright and cheerful but in the evenings we required more light than we usually had especially as Cousin used to extinguish one of the two candles in her desire to curtail household expenses, so she and I sat in semi-darkness at the table until she heard my father's step in the passage, when the other candle was immediately lighted. In those days there were no composite candles, and paraffin lamps did not come into use

---

[42] Jane Taylor lived in Colchester. She is remembered as a poet, hymn writer and children's author and, along with her older sister Ann, was responsible for writing Twinkle, Twinkle Little Star (1806). Prior to this they published the collection Original Poems for Infant Minds in 1804. Hymns for Infant Minds followed in 1808. Their work contained a gentle piety and often provided warnings about behaviour to their young readers.

[43] Olney Hymns, published in 1779, written by William Cowper and the Rev. John Newton. Cowper (1731-1800) was an English poet and hymnodist. One of the most popular poets of his time, but for much of his life he suffered from periods of severe depression.

The Brewery House - A view from the first floor of the house (from what would have been a bedroom window) over the corner of Sun Street and Tilehouse Street.
Photographed by the author in 2009.

for many years after. There were no matches either, save the old fashioned brimstone ones lighted with the tinder cap. [44]

WALKS IN THE HITCHIN AREA

▐▌My dearest father was most indulgent to me. I was always happy when with him and delighted to bound upon his knee, clasp my arms around his neck and cover him with kisses. I often took walks with him particularly in the holidays. Many a time have we gone together to his farm at Offley Grange, nearly two miles from Hitchin. A worthy couple John Lenton & his wife lived there; he was bailiff and had long stories to tell of crops & stock etc. While his wife of whom I was very fond, would regale me with her milk and bread & butter from her dairy.

It was a great delight to me to feed the poultry on these occasions, and visit the pigs, calves etc. While writing of Offley Grange, I am reminded that our two families, my uncle William Lucas's and ours were accustomed

[44]   At this point the manuscript has been marked and a page footnote added thus: *"This box and sulphur caps in my possession 1968 – CLC."* This is almost certainly the Charles Clayton from whom the manuscript was acquired by Hitchin Museum in 1981 and is thought to be Phebe's grandson.

to have a Harvest home party there to take tea, after which we walked perhaps to the village of Offley and visit the church, or in some other direction through the pretty green lanes round the farm, assembling there again to partake of a syllabub before returning home.

On one of these occasions when walking from Hitchin to the farm I was desirous to carry a basket containing the bottle of wine to be used for it, but my cousins Mary & Martha thought it too heavy for me, and were also fearful that I would drop it and break the bottle, but I persisted in taking it, when in a short time the accident they feared took place, and the wine was all spilled. I was very much ashamed & frightened, and thought every body would be deprived of the treat, but I found things were not quite so bad as I feared, for a boy was sent into Hitchin for another bottle, which consoled me, but I have never forgotten this instance of self-will.

Miller Edward "Teddy" Burr of Charlton — a Samuel Lucas Drawing — Hitchin Museum

Another of the delightful walks my dear father & I took together was to see the skating & sliding when there was a hard frost on the piece of water at St. Ibbs Bush belonging to Professor Lax [45] who lived near Ippollittes on the London road. It was not the fashion then for girls to skate and not often to slide, but we highly enjoyed looking on at those who were participant in the art of skating, and could cut figures of various shapes on the ice. Our friend Joseph Sharples was very clever in this way, and was often to be seen there when there was a hard frost.

Another charming walk we often took together was to the water mill at Charlton, a little hamlet on the confines of Hitchin Park. The mill was worked by Edward Burr, his sister Mary kept house for him, simple hospitable folk both of them, and I can never forget their hearty tones of welcome as we entered the house. The great attraction to me was the garden and broad sheet of water at the mill head, where a fine pair of swans might always be seen swimming about, as well as occasional moor hens or dabchicks [46] about the islands further up the stream. E. Burr was remarkably fond of flowers, and succeeded in growing them beautifully, he was also very liberal in cutting them for his visitors and we always returned home from our visits there laden with a handsome bouquet.

---

[45] The Rev William Lax(1762-1837), Vicar of St Ibbs parish with Great Wymondley and of Marsworth Bucks and Lowndes Professor of Astronomy and Geometry in the University of Cambridge. He died at St Ibbs aged 75 years.

[46] Now better known as the little grebe.

Charlton Mill with Miller Edward Burr, 1845. From an oil painting by Samuel Lucas – Hitchin Museum

LIFE AT THE BREWERY HOUSE

❚❚We had two servants who had lived many years with us, Mary Valentine the cook, and Sally Pack, housemaid. I slept in a little press bed in their room in my very early years, they were very kind to me, and after my dear Sarah went to boarding-school, I should have been very lonely but for them. How snug and delightful it was to go into the kitchen before I went to bed and sit awhile in the warm chimney corner, and eat my supper of bread & cheese, or bread & treacle for a treat, while Mary & Sally sat at their work at a little round table close by. A long piece of hopbagging was laid down by the fire by way of a hearth rug, which was a very good substitute for a carpet. Our kitchen floor was of stone kept spotlessly clean by Mary who worked it I believe every day after dinner. There were some deers antlers fastened to the wall, which served as hooks for hats & coats to be hung on and looked quite handsome. I think our kitchen was the pleasantest room in the house. There were two large windows, one looking into the little yard, which opened onto the Brewhouse yard where there was always something going on, and the other into our more private yard, where the counting house was (spoken of before) and from whence we reached the garden by a passage. On one day in the year, St.

37

Part of the Lucas Brewery viewed from Bridge Street, photographed in 1879. The house, No 1 Bridge Street, also known as 'The Brewer's House', was occupied by brewery staff and is probably the one used by the clerk, Thomas Marsh, until he left brewery employment in 1831. It is also believed to have been occupied by the Jeeves family, who worked for the brewery from at least 1841 until 1901, father and son, both John, having served as clerks. The people are stood by the parapet of the bridge over the River Hiz. Unfortunately, their names have not been recorded. The bridge was built in 1784. Hitchin Museum

Thomas's Day 21st Dec until 12 o'clock at noon, this yard was thronged with women & children going up to the counting house to claim the penny which was given to any person who liked to ask for it by the firm, care being taken that only one of a family received it. Of course I always applied for the gift and received it.

I used to be more happy if allowed by Mary to have a broom or mop, and clean a strip of pavement in the little yard, and I always thought I much improved the appearance. We kept a number of pigeons and it was a great pleasure to feed them with peas obtained by going up a steep ladder to a loft in the Brewhouse yard, this I constantly did, and frequently visited the storehouse, walking between the rows of casks, and seeing the yeast dropping into receptacles for it when the working process was going on. There was a slight feeling of awe when I came to the spot two immense barrels or vats stood each more like a house than anything I can compare them to. They were called the King, and Queen, and were reckoned a wonderful sight; we liked to take our friends to see them. They were filled I believe with strong ale. I used often to visit the

Brewhouse also, which was a much more interesting place to me than the Storehouse. There were large places called coolers, it was fine fun to put on a gigantic pair of pattens [47] belonging to George Westwood the brewer & shuffle about in them when the coolers had four or five inches of water in them, another advantage was that when looking through the windows of the coolers, I could overlook our neighbours' gardens, which was very gratifying to my curiosity, and I thought they looked very superior to ours. Then there was the mill where the malt was ground, in which the patient old blind horse performed his endless journey. I often stood and watched him and pitied the poor animal, tho' I must admit that he looked extremely well cared for. We had a pleasant garden at the back of the Brewhouse, laid out in the old-fashioned style, with straight gravel walks, and flower beds either side, a small plot of grass, and a considerable part devoted to fruit and a few vegetables.

My father was very fond of flowers. He always had choice auriculars in the spring arranged on a stand in what we called "The Cloisters", a kind of summer house, roofed but open at the side, with pillars to support it. Several wooden armchairs painted green stood there. We often sat in the Cloisters in summer with our books or work. We also had very beautiful picotees and carnations grown in long beds to themselves, my father being a connoisseur in such flowers people used often to see them when in bloom. In the flower borders we had many moss and damask rose bushes and fragrant cabbage roses, which I used to think lovely, at that time there were none of the beautiful variety of roses that are grown now, but I cannot omit the sweet little Scotch roses of which we had several bushes, and the monthly roses growing up the wall, all of which were a joy to me.

I had a little garden of my own, but as it was shaded by two fine tall Lombardy poplars my flowers did not flourish much but our gardener Frank Smith did his best to help me. We had another garden at the top of a maltster's yard belonging to my uncle & father in Cock St [48] as it was then called, it is now known as High St. I often went there with my father, and at other times with my young companions. Here was a very fine mulberry tree which bore abundance of delicious fruit besides a good supply of the choicer of wall fruit, peaches, nectarines, apricots & white currants also trained on a wall & netted, so that a supply might be forthcoming at our quarterly meeting table in the 9th month. Cherries, gooseberries & currants grew abundantly in this production garden.

[47] Pattens were clogs, overshoes or sandals, held on the foot by leather or cloth bands, often with a wooden sole or metal device to elevate the foot and increase the wearer's height or aid in walking in mud. They were worn during the Middle Ages outdoors and in public places over (outside) the thin soled shoes of the day. The word is probably derived from the Old French 'pate' meaning hoof or paw. Women continued to wear them in muddy condition until the nineteenth or even early 20th century.

[48] At number 11 High Street, behind what is now the Café Rouge.

There was a good sized square grass plot which was well adapted for our favourite game of base ball, as fruit trees were planted on it at convenient distances. There was also in one corner a pretty little thatched summer house where we could sit & amuse ourselves, made this garden a favourite spot in my young days. I believe the ancient mulberry tree still exists and continues to bear a modicum of fruit to keep up its credit, but the garden is quite altered and modernized, the old maltings are gone and in place of the ancient and little butchers shop kept by one Atkins, stands the spacious linen & woollen drapery establishment and commodious house built by the late John Thompson, who married my cousin Mary Lucas, my uncle W.L's eldest daughter.

SCHOOLING IN HITCHIN

❚❚The first school I attended was kept by Fanny Reynolds in Tilehouse St. It was a very elementary affair. I well remember the difficulty of mastering such sentences as "Did he go up", at that school. I remember too being carried to school on one occasion when I think the snow was on the ground by Jervis one of the brewhouse men.

In process of time I was sent to a school with my sister Sarah of much more pretention kept by Mrs. Crosse in Bancroft, (next door to Fred^k. Seebohm's House) she was a widow lady in reduced circumstances and had 3 daughters. The eldest Kate was one of the handsomest young people I ever remember to have seen. I used greatly to admire her beautiful abundant hair coiled around her graceful head. She was always kind to me, but I was in awe of her mother who used to hold my hand rather tightly in guiding me how to form my writing letters.

I remember being much delighted with having a nice warm grey duffle cloak like my sister's to go to school in, they had hoods to them. In summer I think I mostly wore a nankeen [49] bonnet for common, & spencer [50] of the same material. I much disliked the bonnet and avoided wearing it as much as I could. Our best bonnets were of fine white straw with a little white ribbon frill behind and white strings, which with a white frock & muslin or silk spencer according to the weather was our usual Sunday costume during the summer. In winter we had dark cloth peleisses [51] with small capes, and my beaver bonnets and worsted gloves. Even in winter I never had long sleeves to my frocks, though I suffered very much from chapped arms & hands, but it was not the custom to leave off the short sleeves of our frocks till we were 13 or 14 years old.

---

[49] Nankeen is a kind of pale yellowish cloth, originally made at Nanking from a yellow variety of cotton.

[50] In the 19th century, the term "spencer" was used to describe any type of short jacket or coat.

[51] Peleisse (or pelisse) was the fashionable contemporary term for a garment which was half-way between a dress and a coat, and typically calf-length.

After Mrs. Crosse left Hitchin there was no other suitable school for me to attend and Sarah having then gone to Norwich, our very kind friends, Elizabeth & Mary Ransom offered to teach me with their two nieces Maria & Caroline, this was a most kind and friendly offer, and gladly accepted by my father. I enjoyed the time I was with them very much. I suppose it was about a year I was their pupil. I fear they found me very inattentive as I remember the number of tickets gained was too small to merit a prize, but in their kindness lest I should be discouraged they presented me with a pretty little morocco reticule. For the benefit of those who may read this book I may say that Eliz[th.] was afterwards married to Jos[h.] Sharples and was the mother of the late Mrs. Alex[r.] Peckover [52] of Wisbeach and Mary married William Exton, her eldest daughter is now Mrs Gurney Barclay.

Sometimes in the summer while under their care we all went to Grove Mill, about a mile from Hitchin where their brother Joseph carried on a flour mill. He had a very nice house by the side of the mill stream, it was a very great treat to me to go there, lessons went on as usual but the surroundings were so pleasant when lessons were over, the walk by the river terminated by a little rustic bridge, on which we crossed to a little island which we often explored, and in the paddock on one side of the garden a nice little tent was set up, which we often frequented.

Grove Mill, previously named Shotling Mill and then Burnt Mill. This building was completed in 1815. It replaced an earlier one (Burnt Mill) which had suffered fire damage in 1694 but wasn't finally demolished until 1814. Phebe records visiting the mill in her childhood when it was being operated by Joseph Ransom. An old Lucas family tree, deposited in Hitchin Museum, shows William Lucas as being the miller at Shotling Mill in 1613. Photograph reproduced from the Lawson Thompson Scrapbook in Hitchin Museum.

---

[52] Alexander Peckover, first and last Baron Peckover (1830-1919). He was educated at the Quaker Grove House School, Tottenham. He married Eliza Sharples in 1858.

When at Hitchin we had school in the winter in family dining room, a large handsome apartment, and in summer we used an equally large bedroom over it. I have a vivid remembrance of the aged parents of my friends and thinking what a handsome old gentleman John Ransom was, he wore a flaxen wig with a row of curls at the back. He and his wife were mostly sitting each side of the fire while school was going on. E & M. R. were very kind to me, and their influence was so good that it must have been just what I wanted. Maria & Caroline were both older than myself and were among my young contemporaries but Eliza Marsh was at that time my most intimate companion. She lived almost close to us and it was so handy to rush to her house whenever I liked. She also often came to our house and helped me sometimes to make "a feast" with the little toy dinner and tea things.

We often played with my dolls, there was a small cupboard in my brother Joseph's bedroom fitted with shelves, and tiny Dutch dolls with very short waisted frocks lived in it. This we delighted in playing with and it underwent a regular house-cleaning. The little dolls referred to were most of them I believe dressed by my dear cousin Ellen Wright and my sister Sarah who worked under her directions. She was the daughter of William Wright, my dear father's first cousin and was a frequent visitor to our house for weeks together.

We were all glad to have her with us; she was so cheerful and pleasant to all. I was particularly fond of her, and remember her bright face, and dark hair curled in an unbroken roll behind. In after life a closer link united us when I became her sister in law. She was a loving and true friend to me all through the after vicissitudes of life. The present generation will recognise in her the dear "Aunt Ellen" of the home at Leighton. She married your uncle Joseph Glaisyer in 1832. I came over from Lewes where I was at school, and was present at the wedding.

Now we return to recollections of young friends. Eliza Marsh and I frequently joined Esther and Mary Whiting on Saturday afternoons; they were daughters of John & Margaret Whiting. Sometimes we went to Highbury where J.W. had a good sized garden and what then seemed a grand summer house, with windows into the lane at the back. Here we played for hours, always I think under Esther's directions she being the eldest. There were beehives in that garden which much impressed me, and the Whitings had a donkey cart which we were sometimes allowed to use, of course it was very delightful. At other times the same party would go on holiday afternoons to Mount Pleasant, a delightful spot planted with fir trees with here or there a seat or small alcove, it belonged to my uncle William Lucas, and is one of the places near Hitchin connected with delightful reminiscences of my childhood, we had charming views of the surrounding country from the more open walks, and in more retired ones the songs of immeasurable birds. The alcove on our Sat^y afternoon visits was always our home, Esther was our mother, & set all her children in sweeping her kitchen clean & preparing the dinner & other meals.

Lost And Found on the Bedford Road

❚❚Though I had several young companions with whom I mostly spent the Saturday afternoons, I often realized a certain loneliness and longed for a sister my own age. One fine evening I well remember I went after tea to ask Maria & Ernestine Ransom to go for a walk. I was told that the children were all gone to meet their father & mother who were expected to return from a trip to Leicestershire. I at once decided to go myself, and join the party, so set off along the Bedford Road which was the route I expected they would take, and walked on a long way without meeting my friends.

I suppose it must have been getting dusk, for to this day I have a feeling of the sense of desolation that came over me on that solitary road in the waning light. But a piece of good fortune I little expected was at hand. I heard a gig approaching behind me, who should it contain but our kind old friend Oswald Foster, the doctor. He drew up when he recognised the forlorn little pilgrim trudging along towards Bedford, and when he had heard my story told me to get up on his gig and he would take me home. He was going to visit a patient not far off. I gladly obeyed and thus was relieved of my misgivings as to how my walk was to end. I have no doubt that I missed the Ransom party by their having taken a short cut into the town before I reached the turning.

Family Relationships

❚❚No account of my early days would be complete without mentioning my cousin Francis Lucas, my uncle William's [53] youngest son, who was only a few months older than myself, my aunt was most kind in asking me to go to tea with them. He was a bright, clever, lively boy with beautiful large dark eyes and rosy cheeks. He was very fond of drawing. We used to kneel on the chairs in their large bow window of the parlour [54], whence there was a convenient shelf for his book or slate. He used to amuse me much with his sketches of imaginary scenes, chiefly of combats or battles as far as I recollect now.

These drawings were also accompanied by a fluent running commentary on the proceedings of the person depicted. In those days our two families were in the habit of dining at each other's houses occasionally, and a large party we always were, we enjoyed these reunions very much. I think they were very useful in keeping the links of relationship bright, and maintaining interest in each others pursuits and employments.

---

[53]   William Lucas V

[54]   Of the Lucas House in Tilehouse Street

Phebe's cousin, Francis Lucas in 1896 (the year of his death) beside the Cooper's Arms in Tilehouse Street. Lawson Thompson Scrapbook, Hitchin Museum.

In the spring & summer the younger members of the two families frequently walked together in the evenings. I have delightful recollections of walks in the Park, Mount Pleasant or Willow Lane where we were sure to hear the nightingale, Orton Head, and many other spots visited in these occasions. We often fell in with my dear uncle William Lucas who loved a country walk with spud [55] in hand with his old dog Trim or Pepper by his side.

His favourite spot was Orton Head, he possessed some land there, the river was the boundary of one part of it, and a very pretty band of trees planted I believe by him made quite an ornamental finish, here he used often to sit on an old stump, and, unseen himself could watch the movements of the small animals that frequent the water's edge, and of the numerous birds who found there such a delightful and safe retreat to build their nests and rear their young. In later time there was a boat at Orton Head, which gave great pleasure to a younger generation.

---

[55] Contrary to current usage, 'spuds' were various sharp, spade-like or chisel-like tools used for rooting out weeds, stripping off bark or for digging potatoes, and other tubers

Of Aunt Phebe Allen and West Mill

❚❚ By following the course of the stream we came to a common which I found in after years was rich in wild flowers, among them the elegant grass of Parnassus ranks the highest. Many were the rambles we took over that common when our attention had been drawn to the delights of botanical research. Still further through the meadows we approached the head of the stream where stood the water mill, at that time carried on by my uncle Samuel Allen, where I think I may certainly say that some of the happiest days of my childhood were spent; it was the residence of my dear Uncle & Aunt Samuel & Phebe Allen and their five sons. She was my father's only sister, and after my mother's death felt a deep interest in Sarah & myself; & in the summer & winter holidays always invited us to spend a week at West Mill.

Phebe Allen – a drawing by Samuel Lucas.

There was much to interest us there, and she was so bright and cheerful, and found occupations for us of a very different kind from any we had at home. I consider I owe to her influence any little taste I possess in so many directions that I can scarcely enumerate them. She was an ardent admirer of the beauties of nature, and in the summer would take us long evening walks, sometimes as far as Highdown, where the wonderful wide spreading landscape, a few paces from the old house, used always to be a great delight to gaze upon. It was something like the view we have when we are halfway up Wolfstonbury [56] at Hurst.

At other times there would be calls to make at Pirton or Ickleford on some poor woman who my aunt wished to make some little present. I think she never went empty handed to the cottages in the neighbourhood. I was deeply interested in these visits, and it was a joy to make some simple garment for a child under her directions whom we had seen in our cottage visits. I recollect there was a poor family, probably Irish, camping out not far from West Mill in a most destitute condition who enlisted our sympathies, and a great deal was done for them, we made many garments with my aunt, & the housemaid. I don't now remember what became of these poor people. I believe food was often sent to them from the mill.

There was a large garden at the back of the house at West Mill, and an orchard beyond, the river was the boundary at one side. No one could have had more pleasure in flowers than my aunt, she liked the best sorts of every plant, and particularly those which were sweet scented. In summer we were sent after breakfast into the garden, each with a

---

[56] A reference to what is now more commonly known as Wolstanbury, at Hurstpierpoint in Sussex, the county in which Phebe lived after her marriage.

Phebe (Lucas) Allen's Sampler created in 1782 (when she was 13 years old).
Reproduced here by courtesy of Rebecca Scott and Hitchin Museum.

basket to collect the leaves which were past their best, and then spread them on newspapers in the spare room to dry, they were then put into muslin bags, and laid among the linen & caps and handkerchiefs in the drawers. No one could go near my aunt without being aware of the sweet perfume of roses, which with her sweet fair complexion, and expressive blue eyes rendered her very attractive. How delightful it was the first evening of our visits there to go to bed in the charming little room which was always allotted to us, with its snow white bedding and curtains, all pervaded by the sweet smell of roses, which really seemed to belong to my dear aunt wherever she went.

She used to come and visit us when we were snugly in bed, and in her impressive way would read a little in the Bible, repeat a hymn perhaps, and add a few loving remarks of her own. She was always seeking to imbue our minds with a sense of the many blessings bestowed on us, and to raise in us the tribute of gratitude to the Almighty for his good and beautiful gifts. At a very early age I was taught that Hymn of Dr. Watts' which I hope will never go out of fashion while the English language lasts,

"When'eer I take my walks abroad

What shall I render to my God

For all his gifts to me".

& how I should like all my dear grandchildren to learn this sweet hymn while they are yet quite young, they would never forget it in after life, and often would its sweet sentiments recur to them even in old age, as I can testify checking sometimes a feeling of discontent which will sometimes creep in, and raising the heart in thanksgiving to the gracious giver of all the numerous blessings we enjoy.

My aunt was extremely kind to her poor neighbours in illness, on one of our visits to West Mill we were employed in putting up a quantity of powders for the poor, some of whom had ague [57], we were shown how to measure the quantities in the medicine chest scales, and to prepare the papers for folding up in when the ingredients were all ready, this though requiring some nicety I think we did to her satisfaction.

My aunt had a very large handsome mahogany box, much larger than a writing desk, with trays fitted to it, these were filled with beautiful shells, pieces of spar, agates and other curiosities laid on cotton wool. Among them was a beautiful little silver book or case, the lids were filigree work very beautifully chased, it was discovered by workmen in digging foundations for some building; the contents of the little case fell to pieces as soon as it was exposed to the air, so no knows its history. I believe my father presented it to Aunt Allen, and she valued it very much. It was one of our great treats to be allowed to set this precious box to rights, which we did with a soft duster and bit of wash leather, we then replaced every thing with great care, hearing from dear aunt while so employed, the history of many of the treasures. Among them were many curious foreign seed vessels and other interesting relics. My aunt often sketched a pretty wreath, or basket of flowers on paper for me to prick. She did it very nicely with much taste, and I think I did my part creditably, so much did she encourage us to put forth our powers. It was delightful to hear her read aloud, which she often did from a book called "Cottage

---

[57] Ague was an old name for malaria but became a general term for chills or fevers.

dialogues" [58], consisting of conversations between two poor Irish women, Rose & Nancy, one of them thrifty & careful, the other just the reverse, my aunt could give the most amusing effect to their talk, and imitated the Irish brogue exceedingly well.

I remember she often read it to us at our earnest request as we floated up the river in the boat, while the swans would follow us to seize the bits of bread we brought for them, it was so delightful to go in the boat with her on the warm summer afternoons, we sometimes got as far as Orton Head. She sometimes read in "Evenings at Home" [59] "The Colonists", Eyes & no eyes", "The Travelled Ant", "The Transmigrations of Indur" were among the favourites. She was very fond of Cowper's poems, and often read portions to us, I particularly remember the noble lines on Slavery at the beginning of the 2nd book of The Task, she wished me to learn them, which I afterwards did. Lines on receiving

Samuel Allen at a Quaker meeting –From an oil painting by Samuel Lucas Hitchin Museum.

my Mother's picture, Alexander Selkirk, and many of the smaller poems were also among her favourites. It was a pleasure to her that she had once seen the poet when on a visit to her cousins Ann & Mary Smith of Olney.

The baking day at West Mill was a very important time to us, as we then made little cakes for ourselves. I thought it a very wonderful thing to be able to make anything so nice as these cakes proved to be at tea time. Of course there were numerous ducks and chicks to be fed at West Mill. We stirred up their breakfast of barley meal in a great red pan, and enjoyed doing it as much as they did the eating of it. Sometimes I went into the mill and watched my cousin Stafford chipping away at the great mill stones, or placed my hands under the hopper where the warm soft flour was pouring down.

Cousin Stafford used to stuff birds beautifully and I liked very much to watch his proceedings. He was quite a naturalist and knew a great deal

[58] Cottage Dialogues Among The Irish Peasantry, by Mary Leadbeater. With Notes And A Preface By Maria Edgeworth. Published in London: Printed For J. Johnson And Co. St. Paul's churchyard, 1811. Republished by: Kessinger Publishing, LLC (June 29, 2008), ISBN: 978-1436814836

[59] Evenings at Home, or The Juvenile Budget Opened (1792-1796) is a collection of six volumes of stories written by John Aikin and his sister Anna Leticia Barbauld. An 1858 edition is now published on the internet by Google Book Search.

about birds and their habits, a small room over the counting house was used for this purpose. My cousin William Allen was I believe apprenticed to Benjamin Bull Collins at Royston and the two youngest sons Joseph and John, were mostly at school during our visits, and if at home were much occupied with playing cricket, and other amusements that boys delight in. My uncle and aunt were deeply interested in the efforts then being made for the suppression of the slave trade, and were in constant communication with their brother William Allen [60], and his little band of earnest men who worked so hard for this object. One means they adopted to lessen the use of slave grown sugar was to abolish the use of the article as much as possible from the table. I recollect the peculiar flavour given to gooseberry or apple puddings when sweetened with honey instead of sugar.

In our summer visits to the mill we often sat in the spare bed room in the afternoons, it was quite a large & pleasant room with a window in front of the house and another looking into the garden at the back. My aunt used to read to us very often from her vast collection of manuscripts copied by herself or uncle, they were of very varied character, many were pieces of poetry, some of them of rather a jocose character.

I remember it was she who first introduced to us the beautiful lyric of Sir W. Scott's "I climbed the dark brow of mighty Helvellyn", also Parnell's "Hermit", "The three warnings", many of Cowpers smaller and portions of his longer poems, also some of Thomas Wilkinson's [61] whose simple pieces she was very fond of. We were delighted when we could persuade her to tell us what she did when she was a little girl. I wish I could remember these interesting narratives, one thing I can recall. She and my dear father when quite young children went to school together, once he had been naughty, idle perhaps, and as a punishment had a paper pinned on to his little coat behind, on which was written, "idle boy", or to that effect. My dear aunt was so deeply sorry for him that she walked all the way home with her hand over the obnoxious paper so that no one might see it.

My grandfather William Lucas [62] lost his first wife [63] after a short union, she left 3 children, William, Phebe & Joseph. He married again [64] when

---

[60] William Allen FRS, FLS 1770-1843. He sat on the committee of the Society for the Abolition of the Slave Trade with William Wilberforce. A contemporary and colleague of Humphrey Davy, Allen founded The Pharmaceutical Society, later to become The Royal Pharmaceutical Society. Also a great philanthropist, he was responsible for establishing the 'Rural Colony' at Lindfield in Sussex, as an alternative to the 'official' encouragement for the poor to emigrate.

[61] Thomas Wilkinson (1751-1836) was a Quaker and minor poet and writer who was well connected with Burke, Clarkson, Wordsworth and Coleridge.

[62] William Lucas IV

[63] Sarah Lucas, née Redman

[64] To Sarah Camps

I think my aunt must have been five or six years old. In describing her childhood after this event, I gather that she was brought up rather strictly, and in perfect submission and obedience to her step mother.

I have heard her say how <u>good</u> it was for her to have been under her second mother's management and authority. I can imagine that her lively ardent disposition often received checks which perhaps were more salutary than agreeable, but she never spoke of her mother in any but the most respectful terms – and we must remember that it was not expected in those days that children should question, they simply obeyed those who had the rule over them. I think she must have been very sweet looking as she grew up with her beautiful complexion and blue eyes, she was indeed fair to look upon to the last.

William Lucas IV, Phebe's Grandfather. Hitchin Museum

Being so attractive, she had many suitors, some of whom were in very good positions in society, but it was reserved for Samuel Allen a man of insignificant appearance and much marked with small-pox to carry off the prize. She would sometimes tell us a little about these matters when we grew older and I well remember her arch manner of saying in reference to her acceptance of uncle "I went through the wood, & through the wood, and took a crooked stick at last", but after any playful allusions of this kind, she invariably concluded by a warm expression of love to him, and thankfulness for the happiness of her married life, and the help and support that he had been to her.

My aunt was very fond of the society of young people, and deeply interested in promoting their religious and intellectual well-being, but by no means neglected their manners and bearing, and liked to see them neatly dressed

The headstone of Phebe's grandmother, Sarah Lucas (née Redman), is now set into the wall of Hitchin Meeting House. It reads: "Sarah Lucas Died 11ᵗʰ Month 15ᵗʰ 1771 Aged 24 Years". Photographed by the author in 2009

according to their station in life. She was very particular that they should make the best of their appearance by a good upright carriage, and not give way to stooping or slouching which are both bad for the health and mar the effect of the prettiest face. She herself was remarkably upright

Western House in Tilehouse Street, Hitchin. The home of Phebe's grandfather, William Lucas IV, it is now better known as the 'blue-plaqued' house of the Hitchin poet and dramatist George Chapman (1559-1634).
From a watercolour by Alice Lucas – reproduced from A Quaker Journal.

and had a good figure. She was also very particular about clear & good pronunciation in reading and speaking, and I have often heard her lament the mumbling way in which many young people spoke. These remarks apply quite as much to the present day as to former times.

MORE OF THE FAMILY

❙❙There was a large family circle of us at Hitchin in my childhood. I have a very faint remembrance of my grandfather William Lucas. I believe he called at our house every day. On one such occasion I was clattering along the brick passage in my pattens (most likely a new acquisition) he told me to take them off, but even his command was too hard for me, and I still kept them on. It is sad that my only reminiscence of him is connected with an act of disobedience. I was just three years old when this happened as I find that he died in 1819. I have often heard my aunt Allen describe him as a perfect gentleman. He lived in the house now occupied by Annie Lucas in Tilehouse Street [65], where my Grandmother and Aunts Maria & Margaret continued to reside for the remainder of their several lives. We used to go and visit them at intervals and always felt that we must be upon our best behaviour.

---

[65] Western House – illustrated at the top of this page

My grandmother was a tall and rather stately looking woman; she wore old fashioned long mittens over her arms, the sleeves of her gown reaching down to her elbows. She was always seated in a large chair with her back to the window which looked into the garden. I think she sometimes did a little knitting. I used to venerate her very much on account of her great age, tho' I don't think at that time she was more than 82 or 83 years of age. I do not remember that she talked to us children, though I am sure she was kindly interested in us.

My aunt Maria was a very shy retiring person, but possessed warm affectionate feelings, which every now & then revealed themselves. It was a pity that she was so unwilling to show her real loving nature to us, her mind too was cultivated beyond what would be supported from her very timid manner. Aunt Margaret was the younger of the two, both were rather tall and slender — with bright brown eyes and dark hair. Aunt Margaret was a very pretty woman with a clear complexion, & nice colour in her cheeks, it was she who devoted herself to the amusement of her young guests, often playing with us at merrils [66], fox & goose[67], letters & etc. I liked much to go with her into their spacious garrets where the playthings and juvenile books were kept.

I remember some very old fashioned literature which we were very interested in. "The adventures of a pincushion" [68], "The perambulations of a mouse" [69], "The history of the Robins" [70], "Goody Two Shoes" [71], and others whose titles I forget, but they were delightful little volumes I never saw in any other house. There was a beautiful cat at my grandmother's, and better still a lovely little King Charles' spaniel both of them afforded me much amusement, the dog was very snappy to us, though extremely fond of his two mistresses. Their house though very plainly

---

[66] Merrils, also known as 'Nine Men's Morris' is a board game with its origins in ancient history. Layouts have been found on articles, in manuscripts and in tombs dating from various times, including one cut into roofing slabs at Kurna dating from around 1400 BC.

[67] Fox & Goose (also Fox & Hounds) is a board game which is a simplified version of a Scandinavian game dating from at least the 14th century. Edward IV is known to have purchased two foxes and 26 hounds to form two sets of Marelles, believed to be Fox and Hounds. The game was a favorite pastime of Queen Victoria

[68] The adventures of a pincushion designed chiefly for the use of young ladies; In two volumes. by Mary Ann Kilner. Published in 1815, Now published on the internet by http://openlibrary.org

[69] The Life and Perambulations of a Mouse (1783-1784) by Dorothy Kilner, now published on the internet by www.fullstories.net

[70] Fabulous Histories or, the history of the robins. By Sarah Trimmer. Designed for the instruction of children, respecting their treatment of animals. First published in 1786 and now published on the internet by The Centre for Textual Studies at www.cts.dmu.ac.uk

[71] The History of Little Goody Two-Shoes by an anonymous author but was possibly Oliver Goldsmith. First published in 1765 and is the true origin of the phrase "goody two shoes".

furnished, was adorned in most of the rooms with a quantity of very handsome old china. There were three jars on the high chimney piece of the back parlour (or drawing room) which always seemed to my childish fancy to personify my grandmother and two aunts, the centre one being portly and substantial looking, with a rich terra cotta pattern on it, the two side jars were of an elegant and much more slender shape, were dark blue and white.

Then in the summer there was a well kept garden to walk in, Aunt Margaret had very nice flowers in the borders, and in the little greenhouse also. In one of the outhouses was a large old mangle, our linen was brought up to be mangled there after a great wash. There were two sedate women servants kept in the establishment, and a man to attend to the garden, and latterly to drive my aunts out in their little carriage, which was very much like the Victorias [72] we see here. As I got older I became very fond of my two aunts, tho' we always felt sorry that they should live in so secluded a style, as they did not we thought do justice to themselves, they were both of them refined and well educated women and always ready to sympathise in the joys and sorrows of their relations and friends.

My Uncle & Aunt William and Ann Lucas lived a very short distance from my grandmother, also in Tilehouse Street [73]. Their family like ours numbered seven, Mary & Martha, twins, Rachel, William [74], Samuel, Susanna & Francis. They were a gifted and talented family in different ways, most of them being quite beyond the average in power and intellectual acquirements. They were extremely well read, particularly William the eldest son, when we met he almost always had something interesting to tell us of what was going on in the literary world. It was quite a treat to hear him read his favourite pieces from Wordsworth whose poems were about that time becoming very much admired. My cousin Samuel was an amateur artist, and nearly all his leisure time was spent in his painting room. He produced a great number of oil paintings chiefly taken from picturesque spots in the neighbourhood of Hitchin. His water colour sketches of scenery in different parts of England taken when out on holiday were very numerous and most charming. I think they were mostly preferred to the oil paintings.

What a pleasure it was to have such familiar intercourse as we had with my cousins who were not only cultivated and intellectual, but possessed a fund of wit and facetiousness, though it was not until childhood years

---

[72] The victoria was an elegant French carriage, possibly based on a phaeton made for King George IV. It was made some time before 1844, and imported to England by the Prince of Wales in 1869. It was very popular amongst wealthy families. This type of carriage became fashionable with ladies for riding in the park, especially with a stylish coachman installed. It was named after Princess Victoria in the 1830s.

[73] At the Tilehouse

[74] William Lucas VI

Phebe's uncle William Lucas V (1768-1846). From a painting by his son Samuel
— Hitchin Museum

were over, and I was growing up that I could appreciate them, and became sensible to the great advantages of such association, but Francis being so near to my own age was always quite a friend and companion to me; they had a large garden where we played together and a swing in the barn. Our two families nearly always assembled in my uncle's garden after the morning meeting on 1st days. My uncle, like my father was very fond of flowers, and often had some fresh favourites to show us. A few years later he built a small greenhouse, so that he could grow the more delicate sorts of flowers which were quite new at that time. Cinerarias, Primulas, Petunias, and many more.

My uncle was a very quiet and studious man, he delighted in country walks, mostly with his faithful old dog in attendance. He was a close observer of the habits of birds, and other wild creatures of the fields and woods, and was extremely interested in searching for the rarer sorts of wild flowers, so that it became a delight to all of us to find some rare specimen and take it to Uncle Lucas. I fancy that I can see him now seated in his little study (which opened out of their usual sitting room) where he had bookcases filled with his favourite ancient books, some of them of ponderous size. There too he had a cabinet of very valuable coins in which he was much interested. He had also a large collection of old china, managed very tastefully in a little room up stairs. Here I have often seen my cousin Susanna painting flowers from nature, which she could do with great taste.

Both my uncle & father were very fond of reading; he was more retiring than my father, who had much natural gaiety of disposition and bonhomie. Both of them were delightful companions to the circle of young people around them and I believe were much loved and respected by their neighbours in the town, as well as by our more immediate circle of friends. They were kindly and considerate to all around them, & generous to their poor neighbours, sometimes perhaps the latter took advantage of their tender heartedness, for I remember the back doors of both houses were much beset by needy ones wanting a little help, and I believe that they seldom asked in vain.

Phebe's cousin, Samuel Lucas, in 1866.
Lawson Thompson Scrapbook, Hitchin Museum

Of Aunt Ann Lucas

❙❙My Aunt Lucas was very diligent in visiting the poor, particularly in times of illness or distress when she was a firm friend to them. I need hardly say my dear Aunt Allen was very generous in trying to alleviate the troubles of the poor, yet she would sometimes reprove them for coming so often for help, but I believe she could never refrain from a small gift, though she might be well aware of the want of thrift and management that largely produced the need. She has been heard to say to a notorious beggar, "*There go thy ways, here's two pence for thee*".

I remember when a child often seeing Mary Valentine making nourishing jugs of caudle [75] for some poor neighbour when a new baby had arrived, how welcome such little gifts were in times of need; and in more serious illness a slice or two out of the joint at dinner was often sent to a poor sick neighbour from my Uncle's and our tables.

I have written pretty fully of my dear Aunt Allen, but I feel that I must now try to depict somewhat of my dear Aunt Lucas's character, tho' I know how inadequate are any words of mine to describe her. As I think of her now in my old age I seem more able to appreciate her gifts and attainments. She certainly was no common woman, and was much looked up to by all her relations. She possessed a remarkably clear judgement, and was constantly applied to in any trouble or difficult circumstance that might arise. She was so patient and kind in listening to the cases that any of her friends

---

[75] Caudle — a warm drink consisting of wine or ale mixed with sugar, eggs, bread, and various spices.

Ann Lucas (née Bowly).
A silhouette published in 'A
Quaker Journal'

might bring before her, that one felt that she was far from thinking such applications troublesome, but was endeavouring to give the best advice in her power.

She was much valued by all the little body of Friends at Hitchin, and her ministry in our meetings was very acceptable and teaching. She took an active part in conducting the various charities in the town, she and our vicar's wife Sarah Wiles worked in great harmony together, and they had the principal part in the management of many societies, as well as of the British School for girls in Dead Street [76]. I believe my aunt & cousins cut out all the needlework done by the children there.

As I said before, she was a very diligent visitor of her sick neighbours, and she was much loved; and venerated I might say by them, as she could give them much practical advice as to the treatments in illness, and suggesting simple remedies. After my mother's death my Aunt Lucas was our never failing counsellor and friend. I believe she felt that we were left in her charge equally in that of my Aunt Allen and her thoughtful kindness to Sarah and myself can never be forgotten. We lost our dear father [77] when I was just 16 years of age, and Sarah rather more than 20, and her health was quite delicate, so in any emergency or difficulty we had the privilege of my aunt's advice and practical help. In thinking of our circumstance at that time I am ready to exclaim what should we have done without Aunt Lucas? I may say the same of our cousin Susanna [78], with whom a very warm and intimate friendship existed, particularly with my sister Sarah, who was nearer her age. She was a delightful companion, very lively and cultivated, sprightly and witty in her conversation well up in the topics of the time, and clever with her hands as well as her head no wonder she was a universal favourite; she was married in 1838 to Edward Beck of Isleworth, and many delightful visits did we pay her there, and felt that though we had lost this dear cousin as an almost daily companion we had gained in her husband (who was already a distant cousin of ours) a steadfast friend, he was always ready to do a kindness to any one, and welcomed us to his house on our frequent visits with the greatest of cordiality.

---

[76]   Now Queen Street. Ann Lucas was the Treasurer of the girls' school which was established in 1810, foundered and then re-established in1818. Sarah Wiles was the secretary from 1821. Ann's husband William was a 'Dissenter' trustee of the associated boys' school.

[77]   Joseph Lucas died on the 21st 8th mo 1832

[78]   Susanna Lucas, daughter of Ann & William Lucas.

NEW YEAR'S FEAST AND MARKET DAYS

❚❚An important event always occurred at our house soon after the commencement of the new year, this was the men's supper, when all who were employed in the Brewery, maltings and farms assembled in our kitchen, supplemented by tables in the washhouse for the boys, and partook of a substantial meal of roast and boiled beef and mutton, with plum pudding for the second course. My uncle & father with their sons who might be at home, Thos. Marsh, the Clerk, and some of our friends in the town who were often guests at our house, viz Robert Newton, Henry Jermyn, William Brown etc. were always present on these occasions and great geniality and cordiality prevailed.

Sarah Wiles by Samuel Lucas — Hitchin Museum

I used to go into the passage in which were two large windows looking into the kitchen, and watch the proceedings having assisted in stoning the plums previously. When the meal was finished, pipes & tobacco were produced, and the sound of occasional songs reached us in the parlours. The next day the wives of the men had the fragments of the feast distributed to them. Besides this annual supper for the men, we had a large company to dinner every market day, composed of customers from the county round, if they came to give orders or pay their accounts they were invited to dine in the parlour which was of course gladly accepted. Sometimes they were so numerous that the kitchen table was also filled. At any time during the week we were liable to have people sent in for luncheon of meat, bread & cheese & ale in the kitchen, this was sometimes rather inconvenient, but as a child it was quite a matter of amusement to me. This arrangement was altered in the course of a few years when we were older.

Another occurrence which sometimes befell us, and gave me great delight as a child, but which in later years I learnt the great inconvenience of, was, that during thunder storms in the summer when the rain fell in torrents we were liable to be flooded, the water flowing down Tilehouse Street, rushed in at our front door, then came the moment of excitement, would the storm abate before it reached the parlour door, often it held on its way, and then a time of hurry ensued to tear up the carpets so that they should not be wetted. I remember once they were so thoroughly drenched that we had to live in one of the bedrooms nearly a fortnight till they were sufficiently cleansed & dry enough to be put down again.

Visit to Isaac and Sarah Bass at Brighton

❙❙When I was about six years old, I was invited to pay a visit to our
cousins Isaac and Sarah Bass at Brighton. I had not been very well,
& it was thought that it would do me good to have some sea bathing.
Our cousin Isaac Bass was a very old friend as well as a relative of my
father's who had always taken a great interest in advising and assisting
him in establishing himself in business at Brighton, and in due time my
brother Edward was apprenticed to him. By that time he had a flourishing
business as wholesale and retail grocer & provision merchant. He took
great interest in local affairs, and all that contributed to the progress and
well being of the town, as well as supporting schools and other charitable
institutions. In these engagements he was heartily seconded by his wife,
she was a sister of John Glaisyer, who was the father of your grandfather,
and was a woman of much energy and power. They had one son and one
daughter, Isaac Gray [79] and Sarah [80].

At the time that I visited them they were living in Brighton Place, where
the grocery business was carried on, there was no private door to the
house, and all co⁵· I.B's numerous callers who often arrived in their private
carriages had to enter through the shop which was quite a small one,
and odorous of butter, cheese, candles etc. the last mentioned being
made on the premises.

My enjoyment of this visit to Brighton was very great, every thing was
so different from my home in quiet little Hitchin, and then there was
the sea, I know I was deeply impressed by it. Sally Bass was then a little
girl of 3 or 4 years old, so I must have been about 3 years her senior. I
remember her perfectly, what a pretty little thing she was, with rather
long light brown hair and brown eyes. A young Friend Debby Waddington
was her nursemaid, and I was pleased for the first time in my life to be her
companion & playfellow in her nursery, where there was a great variety
of playthings including a rocking horse, and a beautifully furnished doll's
house, with numerous dolls, a pair of doves also had a large cage in the
room. We were often taken to walk by the sea and pick up sea weed, and
the time came at last when I was to bathe. I was much frightened when
the old bathing woman plunged my head under water, and I suppose I
cried and made a great fuss, for I was promised by my cousin S.B. that if
I would be good about bathing she would give me a cherry stone with
one hundred silver spoons in it. So I tried to behave better, and when I
left Brighton the treasure was presented to me.

---

[79] Isaac Gray Bass (1815-1879). He became a leader in Brighton civic affairs and was
      appointed as a magistrate in 1854 and mayor of Brighton in 1856.

[80] Sarah (Sally) Bass (1819-[1869?]). She married at Brighton in 1858, James Thompson,
      a wool card manufacturer of Netherfield, Westmorland.

I believe it was during this visit that I went to spend a few days with our cousins Thomas & Ann Lidbetter at Southwick, (A.L. was a sister of our cousin S.W.) I remember but little of the details of that time with one exception, there were several children in the family, and in turn I believe that every one of us had the measles, of course this delayed my return to my dear Sally Bass, and very glad I was when it was safe for me to join her again.

Being so much younger than my brothers must explain the reason of so little mention being made of them in this little history, but I can recall with much clearness the annual visits of Edward & Charles when they came home for about a fortnight from Brighton, it was a great pleasure to us all, and particularly to me, as my dear brother Edward liked me to be with him, and the games we had together were often rather boisterous. I think Charles found my sister Sarah more congenial, so they paired off together. I believe it was in 1824 that Sarah went to boarding school at Mary Wylde's at Norwich. Jane & Henrietta Foster also went at the same time, they were the daughters of Oswald and Mary Foster, and were intimate friends of ours.

As the distance was great, and no direct coaches ran through Hitchin, they did not come home in the winter holidays so we enjoyed Sarah's company only in the summer vacation and it was a delight to all of us to meet again after so long a separation. She and I became much more companionable as I got older. I was very much interested in hearing her describe her schoolfellows, but what I liked best of all was to hear her repeat long portions of Sir W. Scott's poems which she had met with at school. As we slept together the time for these recitings was when we woke early in the mornings. I was never tired of hearing the early parts of the "The lay of the last minstrel" and portions of "Marmion". I think she could not have read the Lady of the Lake, as none of that charming poem was repeated to me, and I did not become acquainted with it until I was on a visit at Wellingham on leaving school in 1832, when dear Emily Rickman read it to me.

I paid a second visit to Brighton with my dear father towards the close of 1824. My brother Edward had then left I. Bass and was recently established in business at Southwick with Thomas Lidbetter who was in the corn & coal trade. Sally Bass was then attending a day school kept by Mary Binks another sister of cousin S.W. I accompanied her and among the pupils were Mina Kemp & Bessy Glaisyer. I don't think we had many lessons to learn and don't remember much of what we did there, except one day when there was a most fearful storm of wind and rain, so that it was impossible for us children to return home to dinner and we had to remain until it subsided. A great deal of damage was done by this storm, and the chain pier recently finished sustained serious injury [81]. During this visit to Brighton Place cos. S. Bass invited Benjamina & Emily Rickman to pay her a visit. I was much charmed with them, particularly with Benjamina, they made themselves so delightful to Sally & myself, little did we think of the close love and connection there would be between the families, Benjamina having married my dear brother Edward in 1827, and Emily married Isaac Gray Bass several years later.

VISIT TO THOMAS WOOLSTON LUCAS AT GUILDFORD

‖When our visit to Brighton was over we went to Guildford on our way home to see my Brother Thomas who was apprenticed to John Wiblow an ironmonger there. Here for the first time I met J.W's daughter Mary, who was a little older than myself, to whom I at once became much attached, and the warm friendship then begun was a source of much pleasure and I hope of profit also to both of us until broken by dear Mary's death in 1868. Her elder half sister Eli^zth Emma Trimmer also made a very pleasant impression on me; some years after she became one of our family, being married to my brother Thomas in the 5th. mo 1832.

I think my brother must have had much enjoyment in exploring the beautiful neighbourhood of Guildford when he could spare time for a ramble, it suited him well to be in such a locality as he had a great love for the beauties of nature, was quite a botanist, and collected species of many rare plants, was also very fond of birds, and had too some talent in drawing of which he was very fond, and made many water colour sketches of favourite bits of scenery, and frequently expressed in poetry his great enjoyment in the scenes of natural beauty that surrounded him.

His health was not very strong, but he had a kind and sunny nature, and much endeared himself to all who knew him. We paid another visit on leaving Guildford, and stayed one night at the house of our cousin John Lucas at Tooting. He and his wife used occasionally to visit at our house, and though not very much related, a firm friendship subsisted between him and my father. I recollect that they styled each other by the old fashioned title "Kinsman". They lived in a very old fashioned house with a stiff formal garden behind it. John Lucas took kind notice of me, and in the course of the evening asked me if I had ever made a shirt. I was able to answer truthfully that I had and to my great surprise and delight he presented me with a sovereign as a reward I suppose of my diligence.

---

[81] The Chain Pier was Brighton's first pier and was constructed by Captain Samuel Brown RN. It is said to have been the first pleasure pier in the country. It was completed in 1823 and situated just to the east of the present Palace Pier. On 24th November 1824, the pier's toll house was swept away in the storm mentioned by Phebe. In 1896 the Chain Pier was declared unsafe and two months later was almost completely destroyed by another storm. By that time, construction of its replacement, The Palace Pier, was well advanced.

I cannot at the present time believe that I accomplished all the stitching of the garment and of course my governess prepared all the work for me.

At this time I was a pupil at the recently commenced school of Misses Hudson & Crouch which was quite the best of the kind which had then been opened in Hitchin. I remember my Aunt Lucas called on Miss H. and arranged that I should go there and that I should attend our week day meetings on 5th Days, and not be expected at school on those mornings. I must have been there some years, it was really a well conducted establishment and I was very happy there and much respected my governesses. When my Father & Cousin were once absent at yearly meeting I lived altogether at school and enjoyed it very much.

But I fear I was not a very attentive pupil, for I have recently discovered a short sentence in one of my father's letters to my sister Sarah when she was at Norwich in 1824 (which has been unaccountably preserved) and bears witness to the fact, he says, "Thy sister Phebe sends thee her very very dear love. She is as lively as heretofore, mindful of school engagements, as I have not heard of her being kept so much as was one time the case."

I well remember one occasion when I was detained a long time after school, and Miss Crouch was endeavouring to make me comprehend a pattern I had to work on my sampler. That pattern caused me much tribulation, but as I look at it now it appears so perfectly simple I wonder that I should have been so puzzled with it.

There are many advantages resulting from a residence in a pleasant country place. I am sure my brothers highly enjoyed the long walks they used to take, and their games at cricket and sometimes fishing and shooting. They formed tastes which were a pleasure to them throughout life, there was not one of them who was not conversant with nature & the great variety of her aspects. My brother Charles had much skill in stuffing birds, and for many years was considered a very good shot. He

A pencil drawing by Thomas Woolston Lucas (Location and date unknown) — Hitchin Museum

obtained in this way several specimens of birds not very often met with, and we had some of them stuffed in glass cases. Jeffery formed a very good collection of butterflies, moths and insects for which my father had a nice little cabinet made.

I find on referring to a letter of my father's to Sarah at school, that Jeffery left home in the 9th mo 1824, and was apprenticed to Samuel May [82] at Ampthill, a pleasant little town about 14 miles from Hitchin. My father writes, "I think I shall go there with him and return the next 2nd day, it is a nice situation and I hope he will like it, tho' I shall miss his company much." I think it was in the following summer that Sarah & I spent a week at S. May's being kindly invited by his wife Ann May, whose memory I love to recall. She was sweet and attractive both in person and mind. This visit was highly enjoyed Sarah being chiefly with their daughter Priscilla, while I was allowed to be much in the shop with my dear Jeffery. This suited me exactly. I remember helping him (as I thought) to dress the window and other little things.

My father came to fetch us home and he bought some dresses for us there. It must have been soon after my last visit to Brighton that my brother Edward sent me a beautiful doll with wax arms and legs and she could open & shut her eyes. I shall never forget the pleasure it gave me, not having seen such a splendid doll before. I was not able to dress her myself, but my dear cousin Susanna who was very clever and a beautiful needlewoman, and our kind friend Anna Brown between them were so kind as to make her a complete set of clothing and very beautifully they did it. Anna Brown was one of my very kind friends. She often had me to tea with her. I well remember her mother, an old lady entirely crippled with rheumatic gout, but calm and patient always.

Another little incident of my childhood comes before me which was very interesting at the time. A nest of young squirrels was brought to us as a present. As our cat had then a family of kittens the little strangers were put in her bed. She kindly took to them and brought them up with her own little ones.

One or two of the younger squirrels were afterwards placed in the poplar trees in our garden, where they made their home during one summer at least and came for their food to the cloisters where a supply of bread & milk, nuts etc. were always waiting for them, sometimes the pretty

[82] Samuel May was a draper and a Friend. He lived with his family in Woburn Street, Ampthill and died in 1851. Bedford Museum has over 300 letters of the May family, fully transcribed, covering the years 1819 to 1918. There are at least two references to Phebe in the letters:
In 1838 Priscilla Strange (née May) wrote to Ann May "...Have you heard that S. & P. Allen & Sarah & Phebe Lucas are going to occupy Elizabeth Wheeler's house". In 1843 Ann May wrote to Harriet May "...On 4th day we passed a young couple with a view to being companions for life, Thomas Glaisyer of Brighton, & Phebe Lucas − ...."

creatures would come and take a meal with us while we were sitting in the cloisters. We lost sight of them as winter came on, nor did they appear in the following summer. Perhaps they found a more congenial home.

THE WEDDING OF BENJAMINA RICKMAN AND EDWARD LUCAS

❙❙The next event that I must touch upon is my dear brother Edwards's marriage to Benjamina Rickman which it is an unmixed pleasure to recall. The wedding took place on the 25th of 4 mo 1827 and the whole of our family were present, Sarah having come from Norwich for the purpose. She had a pretty delicate silk dress for the occasion, and I had a new white muslin frock, and silk spencer like Sarah's dress.

We made our headquarters at co^s I Bass's, but on the afternoon previous to the wedding drove over to Wellingham, which was my first introduction to that delightful place, and to the no less delightful family who resided there. John & Sarah Rickman, with their eight daughters and one son. (It was my privilege to claim two of this interesting group of daughters as sisters, Ben^ja. and Christiana, the latter being married to my dear brother Jeffery on the 27th of 4 mo 1836. Your grandmother Elizabeth Glaisyer was Sarah Rickman's only sister, so our families have always been very closely connected and united).

I remember clearly that Benjamina and one of her sisters were standing on the front door steps to receive us, she was in a white dress and looked so nice and happy. After tea we walked in the garden, Sarah H.R. was my companion. I was charmed with that lovely place, and the visits to the grotto [83] and summer house, the former was a delightfully cool retreat walls of which were tastefully covered with shells and bright pieces of spar designed and made I believe by the elder daughters and their brother.

From the summerhouse we obtained a very pretty view of the downs, and the pleasant country at the foot of them. There were four windows with a coloured glass pane in each of them which well represented the four seasons of the year. Then we visited the children's gardens, their rabbits, poultry etc as well as their large play room over the coach house. I had never seen anything so delightful and complete before. After a while we assembled at supper, the two lovers were absent and I recollect uncle Rickman who liked strict punctuality was a little disturbed by their absence, but they appeared after a little while.

The marriage took place the next day at Lewes, several of our Brighton Friends were there. After meeting we returned to Wellingham. I don't remember the details of dinner but in the afternoon the younger pack of the company went for a stroll in the meadows, unfortunately in rushing down stairs I slit my new white frock, and was filled with dismay thinking

---

[83]   The Grotto still exists at Wellingham. David Hitchin describes it further in *Quakers of Lewes.*

Lewes Friends' Meeting House where Phebe attended the marriage of her brother Edward to Benjamina Rickman in 1827.
Photographed in April 2009 by the Author

how displeased co.⁵ S Woolston would be, but I was pleasantly comforted by cousin Emily mending it for me.

The newly married pair took their departure after tea for their home at Southwick, and their sister Priscilla accompanied them, Our party remained at Wellingham that night, and next morning were driven into Lewes by uncle Rickman. We made a call at Mary Ann Godlee's as my father wished to become acquainted with her and her sisters, no doubt with a view of my becoming a pupil there after a while. We then returned to Brighton and before going back to Hitchin went over to Southwick to take tea with the dear bride & bridegroom. It was a happy visit, and the numerous presents they had received were displayed for our inspection. I remember there was a good deal of silver among them which I expect was chiefly from the Wellingham family.

As Sarah was to remain in the south until after the summer vacation, she did not return home with us but stayed for some weeks with our cousins I & S Bass, here she was joined by our cousin Susanna and they had a most delightful time together. Susᵃ was clever and very fascinating and I recollect incidents of this visit being talked of at Brighton for years after.

In the course of the summer we had a nice long visit from Edward & Mina at Hitchin, which was considered as their wedding journey, it was not then the invariable practice as it has since become to take a tour immediately after the wedding.

In the following year in the summer we had the pleasure of receiving them again, this time they were accompanied by little Hannah [84] their firstborn treasure, I remember when the coach stopped at our door. I rushed out anxious to be the first to receive such a precious little stranger into my arms. She looked at me if surprised with her large blue eyes, but did not cry at the vehemence of my embrace. She was a beautiful child, I suppose 4 or 5 months old at that time.

It may well be imagined what a difference it made to dear Sarah and myself to have a bright young sister-in-law introduced into our family who was ready to enter into all of our concerns with most affectionate interest and to help in any way she could. She was a great favourite with my dear father and intercourse with Edward and Mina whether at their own home or at Hitchin much brightened the few remaining years of his life.

My sister Sarah [85] had now left Norwich and in the 8th mo of 1828 I went from home to Lewes school under the kind care of Emily Rickman who had been visiting at Hitchin. I slept at Wellingham that night, and the next day took my place as a pupil at the school at Lewes conducted by my dear friends Mary Ann, Rebecca and Lucy Godlee [86].

A fresh stage of my life had now commenced, I was very nearly twelve years old, and on becoming a schoolgirl I must bid farewell to the Recollection of my Childhood.**"**

This concludes Phebe's journal. Her memories of Hitchin must have been bittersweet, having lost both of her parents there at a young age, but she did return to the town after her schooling in Sussex was completed and, of course, would have had the close support of the family, particularly her aunts Phebe and Ann. In 1838 (when Phebe was 22), she and her sister Sarah were proposing to

[84] Hannah was born on 11th mo 12th 1828. She married John Messser Knight, cement manufacturer and later a JP of Northfleet Kent, at Luton Friends Meeting House in 1862. Francis Lucas wrote of the marriage "This is the first of our family to be knighted!"

[85] Sarah married Thomas Benjamin Horne, a GP, in Brighton in 1847. They moved to Newton Abbott in Devon, where he practised. Sarah died there in 1874.

[86] The school for the daughters of Friends was established in 1826 by Mary (Rickman) Godlee at Dial House in Lewes High Street, and continued by her daughters Mary Ann, Rebecca and Lucy.

move into the (unidentified) house in Bancroft, previously occupied by Elizabeth Wheeler, with Phebe and Samuel Allen. It is unclear what did happen as neither Sarah nor Phebe are to be found in the 1841 census for Hitchin but both her aunt and uncle are indeed to be found in the census, living in Bancroft. The next record of Phebe is in a letter by Ann May of Ampthill, where she records meeting Phebe with Thomas Glaisyer in 1843 *"a young couple with a view to being companions for life"*. Phebe and Thomas were married in the following year at the 2nd Hitchin Friends' Meeting House on 11th mo 1st 1844.

After their marriage, the couple settled in Brighton, where Thomas was a partner in the long established Glaisyer & Kemp, druggists. Their marriage settlement, on a large vellum document, is held by the West Sussex Archives at Chichester but no other family papers have been found. Accordingly, it is only from census and birth, marriage & death records that we can glimpse their married life.

Their first home in Brighton was at 18 York Place. The relatively modest terraced property survives and is now a Chinese restaurant. Between 1844 and 1861, Phebe and Thomas had seven children, four of whom, Herbert, Alice, Eleanor and Edmund, outlived them. By 1861, they had moved to 96 London Road, Brighton and that was to be the family home until Phebe died of influenza in 1904. As stated earlier, the only record that I have found of Phebe visiting Hitchin after her marriage was in the 1881 census, where she is shown at Lawson Thompson's house at 11 High Street. Perhaps, because of advancing years, she is not shown as attending the 1896 funeral of her dear cousin and friend, Francis Lucas.

Thomas predeceased her in 1898, so in accordance with her will, and after some minor bequests, Phebe's assets were divided in trust between her four surviving children. Her estate was valued at £10,423 net which, depending upon the measure used, is worth between £800,000 and £4.2 million by today's values. She made additional provision for her daughter Eleanor, the only one of the four not to have married and still living at home. Eleanor was bequeathed all of the household effects and also the sum of five hundred pounds to *"allow her to establish herself"*. Alice and Eleanor shared equally Phebe's articles of personal clothing and attire.

The trustees were instructed to maintain the family residence for a period not exceeding six months for the convenience of Eleanor. The house was sold to the Cooperative Society in 1906 and the site became part of the largest department store in Brighton, but it was closed in 2007.

Phebe was buried at Black Rock Friends' Burial Ground in Brighton on the 6th of the 12th mo; her death was reported formally to the Lewes and Chichester Monthly Meeting of the Society of Friends on the 15th of the 12th mo 1904. Black Rock Burial Ground was cleared in 1972 in a road building scheme for the new Brighton Marina and the burials were reinterred just over a mile away, at The Lawn Memorial Cemetery on the Downs at Woodingdean.

It seems fitting to conclude this chapter with a poem by Francis Lucas (1816-1896), first cousin and dear friend of Phebe.

The Winding Way, from Sketches of Rural Life & Sketches of Thought.

> There's a winding way leads out of town
> By which we all must wend,
> But nobody knows the end;
> Up a gentle hill it climbs,
> Among the laurels and the limes,
> In the moon of May the winding way
> Rings with the nightingale's song,
> In winter's nights with a trip and a skip
> The sere leaves dance along;
> And is there not a sound of grief
> In the trill of the bird and the trip of the leaf?
> Oh! Varied and rich are the nightingale's notes,
> But they seem to flow through tears,
> And the leaves say, "Hush! We are off and gone
> To hide with the bad old years;
> But we're light of foot, and we mean to stay
> Till we've found the end of the winding way.

Drawing by Samuel Lucas — dated 1865. Hitchin Museum

Chapter 6

Biographical Details

Introduction to the Biographical Details Chapter

Much as I would like to, it would be impossible to provide biographical details for all of the people mentioned by Phebe in her recollections and in her family trees. I have therefore included some of the people who were very close to her or those who have an interesting tale to be told. Not covered here are the Lucas family members who were included in *Hitchin Worthies* — William V, Samuel and Francis — as they were described by Hine in a far more eloquent manner than I could ever aspire to. Neither is William VI included here as his life is so well documented in *A Quaker Journal*. I have, however, used passages from his diaries to add to some of the biographies of people well known to him. Sadly, others, who should possibly be included here, have totally eluded my attempts to research them.

Where appropriate, the person subtitle contains a reference to the Phebe family tree in which they are to be found. The trees are shown on pages 92 to 97. In some cases, references to Friends' Meeting Houses, Friends' Burial Grounds and Monthly Meetings have been abbreviated to FMH, FBG and MM respectively.

ALEXANDER, RACHEL (NÉE LUCAS) 1840–1900   FAMILY TREE 5

Rachel Alexander was Phebe's niece. She was the daughter of Christiana & Jeffery Lucas and was born in Bancroft, Hitchin. She married William Cleverly Alexander in Brighton in 1861 and they had nine children.

William was a Friend, born in Stoke Newington. He was the son of a founder and treasurer of the British and Foreign Anti-slavery Society. A wealthy banker and art collector, he belonged to the Burlington Fine Arts Club and was a proficient artist in his own right. Rachel and William were patrons of James Whistler and commissioned from him works which include portraits of their daughters: *Harmony in Grey and Green: Miss Cicely Alexander*, *Miss May Alexander* and *Portrait of Miss Grace Alexander;* and did much to allow Whistler to become established in this country. Whistler also designed some of the rooms at Aubrey House, the Alexanders' Kensington residence.

Probably the most noted of the Whistler commissions by the Alexanders was *Harmony in Grey and Green* completed in 1874 and now at The Tate Gallery. Whistler demanded over seventy sittings from the ten year old girl, each lasting several hours. She later recalled the torture to which she was subjected: *"I'm afraid I rather considered that I was a victim all through the sittings, or rather standings, for he never let me change my position, and I believe I sometimes used to stand for hours at a time. I know I used to get very tired and cross, and often finished the day in tears".* The picture was first exhibited at the Pall Mall Gallery in 1874 and the critics called it *"a disagreeable presentment of a disagreeable young lady"* and *"an arrangement of silver and bile."* Attitudes change and when *The New York Times* reported Cicely's 1906 marriage to Bernard Spring-Rice in Kensington, it said of the painting *"...is regarded as one of the two or three greatest Whistlers, perhaps the greatest of all."*

Rachel died in Kensington in 1900. William died at the family's country house at Heathfield Park, Hailsham, Sussex in 1916, where he fell down some stairs to his death. (It was rumoured that he was pushed by a disgruntled butler.)

Harmony In Grey and Green - Miss Cicely Alexander By James Whistler 1874. Reproduced under licence by permission of the Tate Gallery.

ALLEN, GEORGE 1813-1893   FAMILY TREE 1

George Allen was born at West Mill, the son of Phebe & Samuel Allen. In 1841 he joined in partnership in a manufacturing chemist with his brother Stafford at Ampthill. The partnership was dissolved in 1857 and George continued on his own account, trading as George Allen & Co. He never married and died at Ampthill.

ALLEN, JOSHUA 1805-1853   FAMILY TREE 1

Joshua Allen was born at Woodham Walter, Essex, the son of Phebe and Samuel Allen. In 1831 he married Mary Marshall, the daughter of a maltster, at Cranfield FMH, when he was recorded as being a shopkeeper in Leighton Buzzard. Mary died in the year following their marriage and he married Ann Berringer, the daughter of a farmer, at Northampton in 1834. Joshua was then recorded as a farmer. They had six children, one of whom was born at Hulme in Manchester. In 1851 he was recorded as being a cattle dealer, visiting his parents in West Lane, Hitchin. He died in Essex.

William Lucas VI wrote of him *"Joshua died middle aged, having been very unsuccessful and caused his father much anxiety, being so entirely uncongenial. The height of his ambition was to be a butcher, and have pretty trade where he might kill half a dozen beasts and about a score of sheep a week"*

Ann survived Joshua until 1879, dying in Chelmsford.

ALLEN, SAMUEL 1771–1868   FAMILY TREE 1

Samuel Allen was born in Tower Hamlets, the son of a wealthy silk-manufacturing and devout Quaker family. His elder brother William was an active abolitionist

and noted chemist. When Samuel married Phebe Lucas (1769-1856) in Hitchin in 1803, he was a mealman (a dealer in meal or flour) of Woodham Ferrers in Essex. The couple lived in Essex for almost the first 5 years of their marriage and moved to West Mill, near Hitchin, in 1807.

One Hitchin Friend said of Samuel Allen: *"He was a man of insignificant appearance, and much disfigured with the smallpox. But in spite of a shattered constitution and a highly nervous disposition he lived to be 97"*. A member of the Lucas family said *"People could never understand how he contrived to win the charming Phebe Lucas for his wife"*. But win her he did, after she reportedly rejected 17 previous proposals of marriage. He always wore Wellington boots, a habit gained from his horse riding days, *"into which he gradually dwindled"* until, according to Susannah Beck, *"there is nothing left of him but a Quaker hat resting on a hunter's boots"*.

When at West Mill, he travelled to London each week on business. Whilst riding home from such a visit in 1812, he nearly succumbed to hypothermia during a heavy blizzard. He and his companion were just able to reach Stevenage, where they recovered.

Samuel Allen
"A Quaker hat resting on a hunter's boots" A Samuel Lucas drawing Hitchin Museum.

After the expiry of the lease at West Mill in 1829, Phebe and Samuel moved to a mill near Leighton Buzzard, returning to Hitchin in about 1838, initially to Sun Street, then to Bancroft and finally settling in West Lane (now Payne's Park). From about 1842, after relinquishing his business interests, he and Phebe travelled far and wide in England and Wales, as travelling ministers, *"intent on doing good everywhere"*

Samuel Allen was evidently a man of estimable character. Upon the death of his uncle, Francis Lucas wrote a letter to the Hertfordshire Express, describing his character thus *"In all his transactions there was perfect directness and integrity. No one had even the possibility of an unsatisfied claim on him; he took the greatest care to be before-hand with every demand"* and *"I remember also his buying of an old domestic,*

*at the price she had given for it, a considerable sum of railway
stock which she had bought with his sanction, and which had
become depreciated.*" He was, however, described by Hine as
being *"Positively taciturn"*. If riding afield with his brother-
in-law William Lucas, who was also uncommunicative, the
two would greet on meeting and say nothing again until
they parted! Taciturn he may have been but as a minister
he was not so restrained and at the marriage of Rachel
Lucas and Richard Low Beck in early September 1822,
he preached to the congregation for an hour in the late
summer heat in the old Hitchin Meeting House.

In *A Quaker Journal,* William Lucas VI writes *"I must
say something of ... Phebe, afterwards married to Samuel
Allen. She was a wonderfully cheerful person and from early life
had been a consistent and very pious woman. Her liberality to
the poor was excessive, and I once heard her rating my Mother
soundly for always giving copper. They were infested with
beggars, certainly ... but the entire absence of censoriousness
and the indulgence shown to the frailties of their poor neighbours were noble and Christian virtues and the world will
not be better for losing them."*

Stafford Allen by
Samuel Lucas.
Hitchin Museum

Both Phebe and Samuel were buried in Hitchin FBG.

ALLEN, STAFFORD 1806-1889   FAMILY TREE 1

Born at Witham, Essex, the son of Phebe & Samuel Allen. Becoming a miller
after his father, in 1833, with Charles May, he founded a chemical manufacturing
company, which became Stafford Allen & Co. based at Ampthill and then
London. He married Hannah Ransome, a daughter of the Ransome engineering
family, at Ipswich FMH in 1839 and they had 10 children. Hannah died in 1880
and he then married Emma Meatyard, of Basingstoke, at Edmonton in 1882 (She
was the daughter of another chemist). Stafford was a leading Abolitionist and
a sitter for the painting *The Anti-Slavery Society Convention, 1840* by Benjamin
Robert Haydon, now at the National Portrait Gallery. He was buried in Stoke
Newington FBG.

ALLEN, WILLIAM 1808-1897   FAMILY TREE 1

William Allen was the 3rd son of Phebe and Samuel Allen and was born at
West Mill. He married Maria Darton at Stoke Newington in 1835. At the time
of marriage he was recorded as being a grocer living in Leighton Buzzard and
that was still the case in 1841. They don't appear to have had any children. By
1851 he had become a paper-stainer (wallpaper manufacturer) at Forest Gate
and was employing 40 men. The couple retired to Clevedon in Somerset but

they subsequently moved to Dorking where he died, having survived his wife by 8 years.

BASS, ISAAC 1782-1855

Born in Ramsey, Hunts in 1782, he married Sarah Glaisyer in Brighton in 1812. He was Clerk to the Lewes and Chichester Friends' Monthly Meeting for many years. Isaac was known to be ruthless in business. In *Unknown Brighton* (1926), George Aitchison recounts:

"It was not an age, be it remembered, which was too squeamish about disturbing other people's vested rights. Drastic treatment was meted out to another tenant in this 'part or parcel of land', where Widow Jenkins lived undisturbed. A relative of Widow Jenkins, one Jenkins, the coppersmith, erected for himself one of the freak houses which seem to have been fairly common in eighteenth-century England. To the house Jenkins added a turret, crowned with a cupola. As a supreme distinction, he covered the whole exterior with scallop-shells.

Jenkins, the coppersmith, set great store by his scallop-shell house. Early in the nineteenth century there came along a certain Quaker, a sturdy gentleman of the name of Isaac Bass. He was something of a local Napoleon. He took certain of the ancient streets in this district in hand and drove thoroughfares through them with the ruthlessness of a Haussmann. The scallop-shell house stood in the direct way of one of these new roads. Isaac Bass went to Jenkins, the coppersmith, and bade him name his price for the egregious house. But his 'Prithee, friend' was of no avail. Jenkins was one of the obstinate Sussex breed—the breed whose family crest is a pig and whose motto is 'We wunt be druv'. To Jenkins the scallop-shell-covered house was the acme of the architectural glories of Brighton. Moreover, it was his home. He would not sell. Isaac Bass, however, was a diplomatist, who ought to have been called Jacob. One fine day a smartly turned out coach and four halted outside the scallop-shell house. Jenkins was invited to step inside and come for a drive to London.

Overwhelmed with the honour, the honest coppersmith got inside, and drove in state to London. He also drove in state back again. When he returned, he rubbed his eyes and thought he was dreaming. The scallop-shell house was gone! It had, like the baseless fabric of a vision, faded, leaving not one shell behind. While Jenkins was enjoying his ride in state to London, Isaac Bass had removed the entire house, shells and all."

BECK, EDWARD 1803-1861   FAMILY TREE 1

Edward Beck was born in Dover in 1803, a younger brother of Richard Low Beck. Originally a sailor, his sailing career is recorded in *The Sea Voyages of Edward Beck in the 1820s*. He married Jane Morris of Bucks in 1832. Upon marriage, he gave up seafaring and became a Wharfinger & Slate Merchant, based at Isleworth. Jane died in 1834. He then married Susanna Lucas, a daughter of Ann & William Lucas V and a favourite cousin of Phebe, in Hitchin in 1838 and they had at least 8 children. He died at Isleworth and was buried at Isleworth FBG.

On 1st Month 15th 1861, just two weeks before his own death, William Lucas VI wrote *"This evening came the affecting intelligence of the death of our dear Brother in law Edward Beck which took place soon after midnight this morning.*

Edward, before he married our sister Susanna, was very intimate with Samuel and myself. When we first knew him he was a sailor, being of a very courageous and adventurous nature his friends acceded to his strong desire for a sea-faring life…
He had risen to be first mate and was looking out for an appointment as Captain, when a sudden acquaintance with Jane Morris of Ampthill led to a matrimonial connection. Edward was a fine character with a very nice sense of honour. Impetuous but most forgiving, always aiming at the best way of doing all he was engaged in, most disinterested and ready to serve others, active and energetic, with a handsome and manly person and address. He was a general favourite and his death causes a blank in our circle which will never be filled up."

This is the last entry in the diary.

BECK, RACHEL (NÉE LUCAS) 1802-1874   FAMILY TREE 1

Born in Hitchin, Rachel was the daughter of Ann and William Lucas V and was Phebe's first cousin. Rachel was educated initially in Hitchin[87] and then at the school of Elizabeth Armstrong at Doncaster. Her brother recorded that she became ill with typhus whilst at Doncaster, but other accounts show that it was scarlet fever. Whichever it was, she was seriously ill and nearly died. She left school when she was about 15 and then settled into the practical duties of home life in Tilehouse Street.

An 1811 drawing by Rachel Lucas (when she was 9 years old) Hitchin Museum

The courtship of Rachel and Richard Low Beck is fully recounted in *Family Fragments*. Richard was born in Dover in 1792 and became a Wine Merchant. The couple met in London in the spring of 1818 at the house of Joseph Jackson Lister [88] when Rachel was in town with her parents, who were attending the Yearly Meeting. It is said that for Richard it was love at first-sight. Unfortunately for him, Rachel was then only 16 — far too young for marriage to be considered! It was to be another four years before he finally won her hand, having had to be resolute in overcoming the doubts and concerns of her mother.

The couple were married in the old Meeting House in Hitchin on the 5th of the 9th month 1822. They were to have eight children and settled in

---

[87] 'Family Fragments' (See Sources and Recommended Reading on page 100), records the 'Dame School' as the Hitchin school attended by Rachel but the school cannot otherwise be identified.

[88] Joseph Jackson Lister FRS was Richard Low Beck's uncle. He is credited with developing modern microscopy and was the father of Lord Joseph Lister.

Tokenhouse Yard in the City and then at Stamford Hill, where Richard followed his profession in the wine trade. Rachel and Richard were regular travelling companions of her brother William and are frequently mentioned in his diaries, published in *A Quaker Journal.* In reporting R.L.'s death on the 2nd of 12th month 1854, William Lucas VI wrote *"In him I have lost a most companionable and sincere friend...He was a man of rare industry, great energy and activity, with a quick and sound judgement in the affairs of life; a most kind and considerate parent..."* Both Richard and Rachel died at Stamford Hill and were buried in Stoke Newington FBG, Richard having predeceased Rachel by 20 years.

BINKS, MARY (NÉE WOOLSTON) 1774-1830

Rachel Lucas, at age 20, shortly before her marriage to Richard Low Beck - from a drawing produced by Joseph Jackson Lister, using a camera lucida[89] Richard Low Beck, circa 1818, from a pastel drawing

Mary (Woolston) Binks was born in Denton, Wellingborough, the daughter of Mary and Thomas Woolston, and was the sister of Phebe's 'Cousin Sarah'. Her father was a *fellmonger* (a dealer in hides and skins). In 1795 she married, in Wellingborough FMH, William Binks of Manchester, a *manufacturer of smallwears.* The couple settled in Manchester and had several children. In 1810 she was in Hitchin and witnessed the birth of Phebe's brother Jeffery.

What subsequently took Mary to Brighton is unknown, but is possibly linked to her sister Ann being married to Thomas Lidbitter at Southwick. Almost at the very time of Phebe's visit to her school in 1824, as mentioned on page 57, Mary was allegedly stealing from a lodger as the following was reported in an October 1825 edition of the *Salisbury & Winchester Journal:*

"Mary Binks, a Quakeress, who kept a school and has lived in good repute at Brighton, has been fully committed to Horsham gaol, on a charge of having stolen several sovereigns, the property of Mr. John Snow, a coach proprietor, who had lodged in her house for more than two years. Mr. Snow had at various times missed sums of money which he could not account for, and did not suspect his landlady till lately. A few days since he and a friend marked 45 sovereigns, which he put in his drawer, and he soon missed

---

[89]   A camera lucida is an optical device used as a drawing aid. It projects an image of the subject onto a drawing surface.

Samuel Lucas, William Lucas VI and Richard Low Beck off to the Lakes in a One Horse Chaise — A Samuel Lucas drawing reproduced from The History of Hitchin.

six of them; he obtained a warrant, and found the six sovereigns in Mary Binks's desk. Upon this charge she is to be tried."

Poor Mary was to be subjected to two trials; one by the Society and one by the Crown. The Society reacted very quickly. On the 18th of 11th mo 1825, Elizabeth Glaisyer and Sarah Bass were appointed by the Lewes and Chichester Woman's Monthly meeting to meet with Mary to establish the facts of the case. Mary was evidently unable to provide a satisfactory account of her actions as a *Testament of Disownment* was issued by the following men's meeting on 20th 1st mo 1826. The Testimony is recorded as follows:

"Whereas Mary Binks a member of this meeting by neglecting to the divine monitor placed within her breast has so far deviated from the path of rectitude and honesty as to be guilty of stealing money from a lodger in her own house; and it not appearing to the friends who were appointed to visit her, that she felt the deep contrition and sorrow which such grievous misconduct requires; this meeting feels itself under the necessity of disowning, and hereby does disown the said Mary Binks.

Nevertheless we sincerely wish that by attending to the openness of the grace of God she may be enabled though through much suffering to have her peace made within her Creator and Redeemer before she goes hence and is seen of men no more."

The result of the assizes trial has not been established. She was fortunate to escape transportation and died at Horsham, possibly in the prison there, and buried in Horsham FBG. It is interesting to see that she was buried as a Friend, given her previous disownment by the Society. Mary had been widowed at an unknown date.

BRYANT, EMILY (NÉE LUCAS) 1841-1869   FAMILY TREE 5

Emily was the daughter of Christiana and Jeffery Lucas and therefore Phebe's niece. She was born in Bancroft, Hitchin and was schooled in the town. After the death of her father, when Emily was 14, her mother moved the family to Brighton. Emily married Arthur Charles Bryant (1842-1884) at Esher FMH in 1866 but she sadly died in Kingston in 1869 at the age of 27, whilst giving birth to her second child, Emil.

Arthur Bryant was born in Plymouth, the son of a co-founder of the Bryant & May match company, based in Bow, East London. He became a partner in the company but had died by the time of the infamous match-girls' strike of 1888. After Emily's death he married Elizabeth, daughter of Eliza & William Lucas VI in 1871 at Hitchin FMH and they had two children. He died when living at Oak Hill Lodge, Kingston-upon-Thames and was buried at St James Church, Surbiton.

CLAYTON, ALICE MARY (NÉE GLAISYER) 1851- UNKNOWN   FAMILY TREE 6

Alice Clayton was one of the four of Phebe's children who survived her. Alice married Charles Clayton (1854-1923) in Steyning in 1878 and they had 6 children. E.V. Lucas speaks fondly of Charles in *The Old Contemporaries* and says that he was "*my first intellectual stimulus*". Charles died in Shoreham. It is believed that it was their son, Charles Lawrence Clayton, from whom Hitchin Museum obtained Phebe's journal in 1981.

FOSTER, OSWALD (DR.) 1773-1841

He was the attending surgeon at the birth of Phebe. From a scrapbook by Francis Lucas:

"*OSWALD FOSTER, (from Oxfordshire, where one of the family [a brother], a racing man, but highly respectable, is still or was very recently living.) was for many years in large practice at Hitchin as a surgeon. He took John Dimsdale's business about 1799. His knowledge of diseases was great his perception of it quick — clear — his treatment was allowed on all hands to be very judicious. At one time he farmed a considerable amount of land under Mr. Baumgarter. In his late years he became slow but continued as much as possible to make his country rounds on horseback. About two years before his death (he) was thrown out of his chaise on the Moorhen Hill. Never recovered the effects of this accident. Died of apoplexy 1841. A member of the Society of Friends but not a born Friend.*"

The incident at Moorhen Hill may not have been the first suffered by Oswald Foster for William Lucas V recorded in a diary entry for 6th mo 5th 1831 "*Oswald Foster, surgeon, was much hurt by being thrown out of his chaise*"

Oswald Foster was buried in Hitchin FBG.

GLAISYER, EDITH (NÉE GLAISYER) 1849-1882 FAMILY TREE 6

The eldest daughter of Phebe and Thomas, she married Henry Glaisyer, a lawyer, in Brighton in 1879. Henry was born in Dublin but was in fact a 3rd or 4th cousin of Edith. He practised in Birmingham and the family home was established at Edgbaston. It was there in 1881 that their first child, Constance, was born and died. Further tragedy was to follow as Edith died the following year, probably when giving birth to their son Henry, who survived and is a legatee in Phebe's will. Edith's husband remarried, and went on to become the Chief Registrar of Birmingham. The law firm that he established still survives. A close relationship was maintained between Henry and his ex-mother in law. His son, also a lawyer, assisted in drawing up her will and he was the informant of her death. Henry died in 1904, just two weeks after Phebe.

GLAISYER, HAROLD 1861-1895 FAMILY TREE 6

Harold Glaisyer was the youngest son of Phebe and Thomas and emigrated to British Columbia in 1886. The 1891 census shows him as being a logger and his religion being *"C of E"*. He never married and died, seemingly alone, when farming at Duncan, on Vancouver Island. His death certificate gives the date of his death as 26th January 1895 and the cause as *"Accidental death from exposure to inclemency of weather"* and records that he was a Quaker, contrary to the 1891 census entry.

GLAISYER, HERBERT 1847-1924 FAMILY TREE 6

Herbert Glaisyer was the second child of Phebe and Thomas. He attended a school at Weston Super Mare in Somerset. In 1875 he emigrated to the USA, where he married Emma Plummer in 1878. She was a US citizen born in Wisconsin, and they had seven children. The first, Arthur Reginald, was born in June 1879. In December of that year, Emma and Herbert are recorded as sailing to Liverpool first-class on the Cunard steam-ship *Bothnia* (the hugely rich Vanderbilt family are on the same passenger list). From the distance of time one could draw the conclusion that the proud parents were taking their son to show to his English grandparents, but there is no record of the child in the passenger list.

In the 1880 US census the family is shown as living in Hawley, Clay Co. Minnesota and his occupation being a farmer. It was in Hawley that all of their children were born. In an article discussing a proposed name change for the town, Herbert is recorded as a *"druggist"* and in July 1885 became the postmaster. Herbert shows up on another passenger list in August 1908, on the White Star Line *Adriatic*, sailing from Southampton to New York, travelling with his son Victor, but as the list available to me only shows British passengers, it is not known if Emma was also travelling with them. Herbert survived Emma by three years. Their children (whom Phebe had so much in mind when writing her recollections), and grandchildren, were to spread throughout the US.

LUCAS, ALBERT 1843-1887   FAMILY TREE 2

Phebe's nephew, Albert was the son of Deborah & Joseph Lucas. He was born in the Brewery House and educated at a Quaker School in Thornaby-on-Tees (now in N. Yorkshire). As were most of the Lucas men, he was an enthusiastic cricketer and was invariably first man for the Lucas team when he lived in Hitchin. He made business connections in the north-east and in 1862 became a partner in Caseborne & Lucas, a cement manufacturing company based in Hartlepool, and which was later to become part of the ICI conglomerate.

Albert Lucas Circa 1870   Albert married the wonderfully named Emma Eliza
From a print in the pos- Wilhelmina Scaife, the daughter of a coal agent & ship
session of Kevin Rowe broker, in 1870 at Stranton Parish Church, Hartlepool
(Cousin of the author and and they had 8 children. The couple settled at The
also a descendant of the Green, Seaton Carew, but had moved to Thornton le
Hitchin Lucas's). Moor, North Riding, before his death from pleurisy, at the age of 43, his occupation then being declared as a *"landed proprietor"*. He was buried at All Saints Church, Northallerton. After his death, Emma moved south, finally settling at Binfield, near Bracknell. She died in a nursing home in Reading in 1923.

LUCAS, ALBERT HENRY (HARRY) 1875-1959   FAMILY TREE 2

The eldest son of Emma and Albert Lucas, Harry was born at The Green, Seaton Carew, Co. Durham. His father died when he was just 12 years old. He attended Snettisham Grammar School in Norfolk and then became a poultry dealer in Sheringham. In 1905 he moved to Ireland and was employed by the Department of Agriculture in Dublin and then Avondale House (near Rathdrum, Co. Wicklow). In 1908 he married Edith Speares in the Church of Ireland, Rathdrum. They had a son, John Albert and a daughter, Olive Beatrice, and resided at Corballis

Corballis Castle, Rathdrum Co. Wicklow.
The Irish home of Harry and Edith Lucas (the
author's grandparents) until circa 1920.
Photographed by the author in 2002.

Castle, Rathdrum. He also farmed there from 1911 after resigning from the Department Of Agriculture.

The family moved to England in the early 1920s, Albert having experienced business difficulties during *The Troubles* and he set up as a poultry farmer at Oaklands Farm, Crowthorne, Berkshire. He and Edith subsequently moved to Harrogate where he also farmed and taught at Harrogate College. He was widowed in 1952, Edith having died on a visit back to Ireland. Harry died at Alton, Hampshire, where he had been lving with his daughter for his last years. (The Grandfather of the author.).

LUCAS, ALFRED 1841-1895   FAMILY TREE 3

Alfred was born at Southwick, Sussex, the son of Benjamina & Edward Lucas and was therefore Phebe's nephew. As a young man he was groomed to succeed to a partnership in the Hitchin Bank, following in the footsteps of his father, but neglect of his duties and taking prolonged holidays caused him to be advised by a senior partner (probably James Hack Tuke) to *"make his career elsewhere"*. He met Jane Drewett (who was very deaf for much of her life) when they were both living in Park Street, Luton, and married her in 1866 at Woburn Sands FMH. It is said to be a small world and the Quaker world was even smaller, as Jane was the sister of Joseph Drewett who had taught at Ackworth and was a co-founder of the Woodlands School in Hitchin [90].

Jane & Alfred moved to Eltham in Kent soon after being married, and then Brighton, where Alfred was an insurance agent & mortgage broker but also supported by his indulgent father. Jane and Alfred had 7 children whose upbringing was mostly left to Jane, with little input from Alfred who was more involved in his own interests including travelling at home and abroad and watching matches at Hove Cricket Ground. He was a man of strong beliefs and was a member of the Anti-Vaccination League. He was heavily fined for not allowing three of his children to be vaccinated. He was also a strong supporter of the temperance movement. Very good-looking but self-indulgent, Alfred appears to have been disliked by most who knew him, including his own family.

Although a Quaker, he took an increasing interest in the Salvation Army and attended many of their meetings. He died in Brighton of mouth cancer and Jane survived him by almost thirty years. A full pen picture of Alfred is included in *The Old Contemporaries* in which his son E.V. Lucas says of him *"My father was a spoilt child and grew into a spoilt man, impatient of everything that did not go his way"*. A further description, in a similar vein, is included in *E.V. Lucas A Portrait* by EV's daughter, Audrey.

---

[90] Woodlands School was established in Bancroft, Hitchin. In the original prospectus published in 1873, it was to be for the sons of Friends. However, a subsequent prospectus, published shortly before opening, had dropped all reference to Friends and it was promoted as a "Select School for Boys" with the fees being reduced from 60 guineas to £20 per annum

LUCAS, ANN (NÉE BOWLY) 1769-1853   FAMILY TREE 1

Born into a noted Cirencester Quaker family, Ann ran a school there until she married William Lucas V at Cirencester FMH in 1798 and they had 11 children. She was a Quaker minister for over 50 years and a clerk to the woman's yearly meeting for 14 years. She is mentioned several times by Hine in *The History of Hitchin*. In addition to the description provided by Phebe, a very full pen picture is provided by her son William Lucas VI, in *A Quaker Journal*. Ann was buried in Hitchin FBG.

LUCAS, CHARLES 1805-1877   FAMILY TREE 2

Charles Lucas "The Bird Stuffer" from a Samuel Lucas drawing in Hitchin Museum

An elder brother of Phebe, born at the Brewery House, Charles was apprenticed to John Glaisyer in Brighton (Phebe's future father-in-law) as a chemist (druggist). His transfer certificate from Hitchin MM was accepted by Lewes and Chichester MM on 12th of 12th mo 1820. He completed his apprenticeship and returned to Hitchin in 1827. In 1839 he was recorded as being a chemist and drug agent, living in Sun Street. He never married and in 1841 was still living in Hitchin and of independent means. His interest in taxidermy, as mentioned by Phebe, lasted for his whole life.

His nephew, E. V. Lucas, referred to him as *"a bird stuffer"* and wrote *"Of this uncle Charles, who never married and spent his last years in retirement at Brighton, near his brother Edward's in Buckingham Road, I have only a very dim memory. I can recall his white hair, his housekeeper Rhoda, his small dog and the atmosphere of desiccated birds and butterflies in which he lived"*. Charles had moved from Hitchin to Brighton by 1861.

LUCAS, CHARLES CECIL 1844-1898   FAMILY TREE 2

The son of Deborah and Joseph Lucas, he was born at the Brewery House and educated at Grove House Quaker School at Tottenham Green, subsequently becoming a solicitor, practising in the firm of Dickson & Lucas of Bedford Row, London. In 1871 he was residing with his parents at Oakfield House, St Ippollitts but emigrated to New Zealand in the mid-1870s where he became a Justice of the Peace. He never married and died in Gisborne NZ.

LUCAS, EDWARD 1803-1874   FAMILY TREES 2 AND 3

Edward was the son of Hannah and Joseph Lucas, so was an elder brother of Phebe. After schooling in Hitchin, he was indentured in 1819 to Isaac Bass at Brighton for seven years *"to be instructed in the art of a tallow chandler and grocer"*. Edward did not complete his apprenticeship. This is unsurprising as his grandson, E.V. Lucas, wrote of Edward's character in *The Old Contemporaries*:

"To Edward Lucas there could be nothing more distasteful than such inconsiderate high-handedness as Bass had practised; he was no overrider of other people's rights, no seeker of wealth or power, although a certain amount of wealth came to him."

In the 1820s, his father bought for him the shipping and wharfinger business of Thomas Lidbetter at Southwick, he thus became a merchant, ship-owner and developer of Shoreham Docks, although in the 1851 census, he listed himself simply as *"a corn and coal merchant"*. Phebe also invested in the business and in 1844 is shown as having shares worth £600. In 1827 Edward married Benjamina Rickman, daughter of John Rickman, at Lewes Friends' Meeting House, and they had 9 children. Their intention to marry was announced at the Lewes and Chichester MM on the 16th of the 3rd mo 1827. Sarah Bass and Elizabeth Glaisyer were appointed to attend the wedding and subsequently reported that *"good order was maintained"* (this was standard procedure for all Quaker weddings). In 1852, Edward sold his interests at Southwick to Robert Horne Penney, who was soon to become his son-in-law, and became a partner in the Hitchin Bank, initially at Hitchin but then settling in Luton, before returning to Sussex in retirement. He died in Brighton, survived by Benjamina by seven years.

LUCAS, EDWARD VERRALL CH (COMPANION OF HONOUR) 1932; HON. DLITT (OXFORD); HON. LLD (ST ANDREWS) 1868-1938   FAMILY TREE 3

Edward Verrall Lucas was born at the Villa Stresa in Eltham, Kent, the second son of Jane (née Drewett) and Alfred Lucas. The family moved to Brighton not long after he was born and he always declared himself to be a *Sussex Man*. Devoted to his mother, who encouraged his taste in literature, he had less affection for his father, whose laxity in financial matters led to Edward being placed in nine different schools, including a few terms at Ackworth, before being apprenticed, aged sixteen, to a bookseller in Brighton.

In 1889 he joined the staff of the *Sussex Daily News* and his first volume of poetry, *Sparks from a Flint*, was published the following year. His literary skill convinced a Drewett uncle to donate £200 for him to attend lectures at University College, where he read assiduously and founded two university magazines. In 1893 he was recruited to *The Globe*, a leading evening paper. An un-demanding work schedule allowed him to spend most of his time in the reading room of the British Library, which he later called his *alma mater*.

A cricket match at Darwin's Downe House in 1913.
E.V. Lucas is 2ⁿᵈ from the right, centre row, his brother Percy and daughter Audrey are in the front row, 1st and 2nd from left. In the photograph are some notable figures of the literary and artistic world of the early 20th century, including A.A Milne (centre row, 1st left) and J.M. Barrie (centre row, 3rd from left). E.V. and James Barrie were the opposing captains. Barrie had formed his 'hapless' team of literary players, 'The Allahakbarries', in 1890. They were disbanded in 1913 and this may well have been their last match. At this time Downe House was being used as a school and Audrey Lucas was a pupil. Author's Collection.

In 1892, the Society of Friends asked him to write a book on Charles Lamb, as well as one on Bernard Barton [91] and to edit a Quaker magazine *The Essayist*. His success in these endeavours led to a commission for *Charles Lamb and the Lloyds* [92] and later, from Methuen, for a new edition of Lamb [93].

He married (Florence) Elizabeth Gertrude Griffiths a daughter of a colonel in the United States army in 1897 and the couple had one daughter, Audrey. Elizabeth was a talented author, writing under the name Mr C. Greene and was a close friend of J. M. Barrie. Edward published parodies of well-known literary works and his growing reputation as a humorist gained him a position at Punch in 1904, where he remained for thirty years. He became noted as a travel writer and wrote articles on India, Japan, and Jamaica and also *A wanderer's notebook* for the Sunday Times. Attempts to turn playwright, in collaboration with Barrie, proved to be unsuccessful. He wrote on a variety of subjects but is now mostly remembered for his essays on cricket.

In 1915 Edward and Elizabeth were given £2000 by 'Jimmy' Barrie to help children in France. They set up a clearing house, come hospital, in a semi-derelict chateau at Bettancourt in the Marne, for children who had been displaced by the war. Edward is said to have been very popular with the children who called him 'Papa Lucas'.

[91] Bernard Barton (1784-1849) known as the 'Quaker Poet'.

[92] Charles Lamb & The Lloyds Published by Smith, Elder & Co. 1898.

[93] Life of Charles Lamb published by Methuen & Co. 1905.

In 1924 he became chairman of the Methuen publishing company, with which he had long been connected. He received the honorary degree of LLD from the University of St Andrews and DLitt from the University of Oxford and was appointed a Companian of Honour in 1932. Throughout his life he had a total of 180 works published. He died in London and was warmly eulogized by his daughter, Audrey, and by A. A. Milne. For some time he had paid for the upkeep of Charles Lamb's grave, and when he died he left a sum for that purpose in perpetuity.

LUCAS, JEFFERY 1810-1855   FAMILY TREE 5

Jeffery Lucas was born at the Brewhouse, a brother of Phebe. After completing his apprenticeship with Samuel May at Ampthill he became a partner in the Hitchin Bank which he appears to have served quietly but loyally until his death at the comparatively young age of 45. As recorded by Phebe, he married Christiana Rickman of Wellingham, at Lewes FMH in 1836 and returned to Hitchin with his bride. They had four children, two of whom married very well; Rachel into the Alexander banking family (see page 64) and Emily into the Bryant family (of the Bryant & May matchmaking company). Christiana appears to have become unsettled after Jeffery's death and lived variously in Brighton and Kingston (Surrey), but she died in Hitchin in 1874, having survived Jeffery by nineteen years. Both were buried in Hitchin FBG.

LUCAS, JOSEPH 1771-1832   FAMILY TREE 2

Phebe's father, he was the son of Sarah (née) Redman and William Lucas IV and born in Hitchin on 8th of the 9th month, 1771. His mother died nine months after his birth, having had three children.

Joseph married Phebe's mother, Hannah Woolston at Finedon Friends' Meeting House, Irthlingborough in 1798. She was born in 1776 at Irthlingborough. He was a banker and active partner (with his elder brother William V), in the Lucas Brewery and gave the impression of being richer than he was, not in an ostentatious way but by virtue of his charity. In *A Quaker Journal*, William Lucas VI wrote that he was "*Kind and indulgent to excess*" and that "*... his religious principles were good and his conduct most upright and honourable.*" However, he does not appear to have been troubled by the *burden* of being involved with the brewing trade and remained in it until his death.

Of Christmas suppers at the Brewhouse, William wrote: "*Those bounteous Christmas suppers in the Brewhouse kitchen, 'when jokes much older than the ale went round,' when my Uncle's merry laugh shot mirth through all the party, and masters, men and tradesmen of the town met in a very free and primitive spirit, would be quite impossible in the present.* Of Joseph's relationship with his men, William wrote "*My Uncle was too familiar with his men. Sometimes in the afternoon I have heard shouts of laughter proceeding from a group collected round him near the copper fire, at his funny stories. I once observed to my Father that I thought him too familiar*

Joseph Lucas (Jnr) in 1866
Lawson Thompson
Scrapbook – Hitchin
Museum

with the workmen. 'Yes,' was his reply, 'but there is no one they are all so willing to serve'.

Hannah died in 1823. Both she and Joseph were buried in Hitchin FBG.

LUCAS, JOSEPH 1801–1877   FAMILY TREE 2

Born in 1801 at the Brewery House in Sun Street, the son of Joseph & Hannah Lucas and was Phebe's eldest brother. In an entry in *A Quaker Journal* for 10th month 23rd 1837, William Lucas remarks "*Symptoms of matrimonial tendencies in our cousin Joseph in sundry mysterious disappearances to Northamptonshire. May they increase till the complaint is fully developed*'.

Joseph (who later became known as 'Old Joe') married Deborah Cooke, the daughter of a farmer of Irchester, at Wellingborough FMH in the following year. They lived at the Brewery House where all of their 8 children were born, but by 1861 had moved to his new house, Oakfield at St Ippollittes (now Kingshott School). It was around that time that Joseph retired from brewery affairs and none of his sons followed him into the trade. Indeed, they all pursued careers away from Hitchin.

Matilda Lucas provides a glimpse of his character: "*[Joseph and Deborah] were both very kind and hospitable, though Joseph could be firm and say 'The omnibus will call for thee in ten minutes' to a relative who had outstayed their welcome*". Joseph owned 17 public houses which had been on lease to the Lucas Brewery and several of which were purchased by Samuel Lucas in an auction sale in 1883 when Joseph's estate was being wound up. Hannah died in 1871. Lifelong Quakers, both were buried in Hitchin FBG.

LUCAS, PERCEVAL DREWETT 1879–1916   FAMILY TREE 3

Born in Itchinfield, Sussex, the son of Alfred & Jane Lucas and a brother of Edward Verrall, Percy Lucas attended Mill Hill School for just the1895 academic year (The short attendance there is probably accounted for by his father not having paid his school fees! A problem also experienced by his brother E.V.). In 1901, Percy was employed as a gardener near Aberystwyth but was also an expert genealogist and in 1911 was recorded as an antiquarian author. He was also an enthusiastic morris man. In 1907 he married Madeleine Meynell, (a daughter of the writer and critic Wilfred Meynell and his wife Alice née Thompson, the poet and essayist) and they had three children, the first of whom was Sylvia, born in1908.

In *England, My England*[94], by D. H. Lawrence, the fictional *Evelyn* is generally thought to be based upon Perceval in an unflattering short story where *Joyce* (Sylvia) falls upon a sickle and is permanently crippled. The accident did happen but in the story Lawrence attributes it to the girl's father's negligence, whereas Percy was abroad at the time that it actually took place. Lawrence also wrote that *Evelyn* (renamed *Egbert* in later publications) was driven to the war by the unhappiness of his marriage. The idea that the story was based upon Percy's family was largely refuted in *D. H. Lawrence, 1885-1930: The Cambridge Biography*. It is surprising, then, that upon hearing of Percy's death on the Somme, Lawrence should write "*It upsets me very much to hear of Percy Lucas. I did not know he was dead. I wish that story at the bottom of the sea, before ever it had been printed.*"

Percy Lucas circa 1915 — Reproduced here by kind permission of Mill Hill School.

Enlisting in September 1914 as a private in the Royal Fusiliers, Percy was commissioned on 17th June, 1915 and joined the Border Regiment. He served with the 2nd Battalion of the regiment and died at Abbeville on 6th July 1916, as a result of wounds received near the village of Fricourt on July 1st — the disastrous first day of the Somme Offensive.

LUCAS, THOMAS WOOLSTON 1807-1881   FAMILY TREE 4

Thomas was born in Hitchin, the son of Joseph and Hannah Lucas and an elder brother of Phebe. His Quaker birth record shows Oswald Foster, Susannah (Camps) Lucas and Ann Lucas as witnesses. He was apprenticed to John Wiblow at Guildford, an Ironmonger. In 1825, Ann May wrote "*Hast thou heard that O. Foster's family have all been ill with a fever, as it was said, & now turns out to have been the small pox, Thomas Lucas (J's brother) has also had it at Guildford*". Thomas married Elizabeth Emma Trimmer at Guildford FMH in 1832 and at that time was recorded as an Ironmonger of Chichester. They had at least seven children. By 1841 the family had moved to Northampton where Thomas was shown as a *Cornfactor* (corn merchant). By 1851 he had become a Chief Clerk in an iron foundry in Luton and remained as such for the remainder of his working life. Thomas retired to Brighton, where he died, having survived Emma by 18 years.

---

[94] England, My England is the title of a collection of short stories which were originally written between 1913 and 1921 and mostly published in magazines. After extensive rewriting by Lawrence, they were published in a single volume in the USA in 1922, a British version followed in 1924. The book is now available online at Project Gutenberg – http://www.gutenberg.org/etext/8914

Lucas, William IV 1744-1819   Family Tree 1

Phebe's grandfather, he was the son of Phebe (née Gray) and William Lucas III. He married Sarah Redman of Earith Huntingdonshire in 1767 at St Ives Friends' Meeting House and they had 3 children, the last being Phebe's father, Joseph. Sarah died in 1771 at the age of 24 and he then married Susannah Camps of Chatteris, Isle of Ely in 1773 *"a truly valuable & comfortable connexion"* according to William Lucas V. They had two children. William died in September 1819, when Phebe was 3 years old, and was buried in FBG Hitchin.

In a diary entry for the 9th of 9th month 1819, William Lucas V recorded the death of his father:

"This day not soon to be forgotten by us, at about ½ past five in the morning, died our dear and honoured father aged 75 years & about 4 months...

He was born on the 31st of the 5th month 1744. He was left the Brewhouse estate & other property in land by his grandfather & at the age of 7 years lost his father: he was at school first at Hemel Hempstead with Thos. Squire, & afterwards at Tottenham with Josiah Forster, & after finishing school did not serve any regular apprenticeship but was placed out in situations merely to fill up the time till he came of age – soon after which he entered into partnership in the Brewery with his uncle I. Gray – who died in Ireland on a religious visit in the year 1784, the business becoming wholly my fathers – he always spoke of his uncle I. Gray in terms of great affection. I think about the year 1796 my father wholly declined business in favour of my Brother & myself & leaving the Brewhouse went to reside at his house in the upper part of Tilehouse Street.

In his character he may be firstly considered as a man of great piety & humility... a very diligent attender of our meetings for worship & discipline, even under bodily indisposition. He had a watchful care over his words and actions – he was a man of very industrious habits & had great aversion to indolence & procrastination in others. His practice was until near the last to rise at about 6 o'clock in Summer & in Winter. He was neat in his person & was neat very exact & punctual in his accounts... In his person he was under the middle size of a spare make, yet not naturally deficient in bodily strength — judging from some instances which I have heard him mention & which exceeded what I was ever able to do. His countenance was expressive, the nose rather large inclining to the aquiline".

Niblock, Joseph White, The Reverend Doctor 1786-1842

A Doctor of Divinity, Joseph Niblock was Master of the Hitchin Free School from 1819 until resigning in 1830. He is credited with making many improvements, but his tenure was accompanied by much controversy within the school and the town. Described as being one of the best Greek scholars in England, he later had published a Greek Grammar [95], used for many years at Eton and other public schools, and also in 1836 *The New Improved Classical Latin and English Dictionary.* Unsurprisingly, he had no interest in providing an elementary education, which had been the previous focus of the school, and certainly not

---

[95]   An elementary treatise on Greek grammar. Now available on-line in Google Book Search.

"to the sons of labourers", i.e. non-fee paying boys, and moved the curriculum towards an emphasis on the Classics and favoured paying pupils.

He was also a strict disciplinarian and probably not the person to be teaching Jeffery, the *"gentle and affectionate"* brother of Phebe (see page 32). In *The History of Hitchin*, Hine announced that Niblock was to be one of his forthcoming *Hitchin Worthies*, but in the event he was not included. Perhaps, upon reflection, Hine decided that given his teaching methods, Niblock was not a suitable subject, for in the chapter on Francis Lucas in *'Worthies'* he wrote *"[Niblock] knew as well as any pedagogue in the land how to drub the Classics into that mulish animal, the English boy. But even Niblock's 'teaching and beating' failed to break the spirit of young Francis…"*

Joseph Niblock died in Sheffield in 1842, the same year that his daughter Amelia St. John married into the aristocratic Wellesley family.

Dr Joseph White Niblock. From a drawing in the Lawson Thompson scrapbook in Hitchin Museum.

RICKMAN, JOHN 1774-1859

John Rickman was born in Lewes and also died there. He owned the Bear Brewery in Lewes and married Sarah Horne at Arundel Friends' Meeting House in 1797; they were to have 9 children (eight daughters and one son!). Two of the daughters became sisters-in-law to Phebe. He was a Quaker who was very successful but very ruthless in business. In *The Old Contemporaries*, his great-grandson E. V. Lucas provides the following anecdote.

"In the eighteen-forties John Horne was an inmate of John Rickman's house at Wellingham, learning the business of malting and brewing which was carried on at Lewes. It was many years later, but with a clear Quaker-like brain, that he recalled for me one of the examples of blended unimaginative precision and tyranny of which John Rickman was capable.

Let John Horne be the narrator and we will call the debtor Richard Blackman.

Richard Blackman, having at last succeeded in amassing the amount of his final obligation, £100, had arranged to be at Mr. Rickman's Lewes office at twelve o'clock next market day, to hand it over and get his quittance.

'Twelve o'clock came'—John Horne is speaking—'and there was no Richard Blackman.

"Let us start now," said John Rickman, as the horse was ready.

"Won't thee give him another five minutes?" I pleaded.

"Let us start now," said John Rickman, gathering up the reins.'

As we were crossing the bridge, who should run up to the gig but Richard Blackman?

"I am very sorry, Mr. Rickman," he said, "but I was detained. I couldn't get here before."

John Rickman pulled out his watch. "I can remember no appointment with any one on Lewes Bridge at five minutes past twelve," he replied.

"But here is the money, Mr. Rickman," said Blackman, proffering a bag.

"I cannot do business on Lewes Bridge," replied the maltster. "I will see thee in my office at twelve o'clock next market day": and he whipped up the horse and was off.

"John," he said, turning to me, "when we get home thee must take thy slate and work out what is a week's interest on £100 at five per cent."

SHIBLEY, MARY JOSEPHINE (NÉE LUCAS) 1839-UNKNOWN   FAMILY TREE 2

Phebe's niece, Mary was the daughter of Deborah and Joseph Lucas and was born at The Brewery house. She married Nassib Abdoullah Shibley at Hampstead in 1887, she being 48 and he 21! It is not a surprise to find that the marriage was very brief as on 2nd January 1889, she paid him £300 (at least £25,000 by current values) under a Deed of Separation, in which he is described as a *"Gent"*. Six years later, in 1893, at the Central Criminal Court, a certain Nassib Abdoolah [sic] Shibley (27), of 54 Parliament Hill Road, Hampstead Heath, pleaded guilty to unlawfully obtaining £6 9s from Margaret Curtis Bevan, and others, by false pretences and was sentenced to ten months hard labour.

It would appear that Shibley left for the United States soon after being released from prison as in 1900 a Nassib A. Shibley (of the correct age) was granted US naturalisation, having entered the country in 1894. The fate of Mary after the separation has not been established.

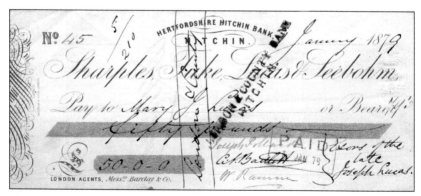

A cheque for the sum of £50-0-0 (about £3500 by today's values), drawn on the Hitchin Bank (Sharples, Tuke, Lucas & Seebohm) from the estate of the late Joseph Lucas, in January 1879, to his daughter, Mary J. Lucas. The signatories are the executors of the estate – Joseph Pollard, Charles Archibald Bartlett and William Ransom. In the possession of the author.

THOMPSON, JOHN 1797-1877   FAMILY TREE 1

When Reginald Hine was selecting those to be included in *Hitchin Worthies*, John Thompson must have surely been a very close contender. Instead, Hine chose to recall three of the children of John and his wife Mary, in a chapter entitled *The Thompsons of Elmside*.

Although he only moved to Hitchin in his early twenties, John very soon became an active and valued citizen; in business, as a Friend and in civic affairs. He was born in Nether Compton in Dorset and was the youngest son of the proprietor of Compton School, a Quaker establishment of high repute and which had some notable alumni. On completing his education, John was apprenticed to an establishment in Wiltshire which had several trades including grocery, draper, printing and bookbinding. He then gained employment with the Jermyn family who were drapers, initially at Baldock and then in 1819 to their premises at 10 Cock Street in Hitchin. In due course, John became the proprietor of the Jermyn firm. He married Mary, the eldest daughter of William V and Ann Lucas, in 1830 and in 1834 moved the drapery business and family home to the adjoining property at no. 11, which had been built for him by his father-in-law. John and Mary had seven children, four of whom survived to adulthood: Mary, Lawson, Catherine & Margaret.

Among his many achievements, John was a founder member of Hitchin Mechanics' Institute; he was a founder trustee of the British and Foreign Schools and he managed the depository of the British and Foreign Bible Society. He is also credited with purchasing the first chimney sweeping machine in the Hitchin area, his aim being to ease the burden of the climbing boys who were so cruelly employed in the trade. He was an avid collector of all manner of things and started the scrapbooks, continued by his son Lawson, which are now a treasured resource in Hitchin Museum. He was a great correspondent and a collection of letters (1840-1874) between John and Thompson cousins in the US is deposited in the Haverford College Library in Pennsylvania.

Mary Thompson died in 1876 and in an obituary for John, she was described thus: *"A lady whose great knowledge of the poor of Hitchin, and her ever ready benevolence in assisting them will be long remembered among us."* Matilda Lucas described John: *"Uncle Thompson was not at all handsome but in his velvet caps would have looked well in a Dutch interior".* He died a year after Mary and both were buried in Hitchin FBG. After his death, an old resident of the town said of him *"I have known Mr Thompson from my childhood, but I have never known him say an unkind thing of anyone nor allow such a thing to be said in his presence without censure or qualifying remark."*

It is very sad that none of their children married and so left no descendants of this esteemed family.

Appendix A

The Descent of the Lucas Family

This Lucas family tree was published in *The Quaker Diaries*. In addition to the six successive eldest Williams shown in it, there were two further ones; William VII (1832-1914) was the last William to serve in the brewery and lived at *The Firs* in Bedford Road (now the Firs Hotel). William VIII (1866-1940) was a stockbroker who lived away from Hitchin. He did marry but the couple had no children and thus ended a tradition that had continued for eight generations.

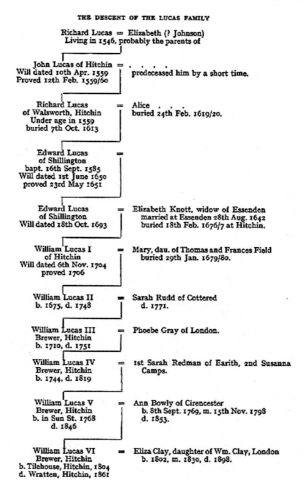

THE DESCENT OF THE LUCAS FAMILY

Richard Lucas = Elizabeth (? Johnson)
Living in 1546, probably the parents of

John Lucas of Hitchin = ...
Will dated 10th Apr. 1559
Proved 12th Feb. 1559/60   predeceased him by a short time.

Richard Lucas = Alice . . .
of Walsworth, Hitchin   buried 24th Feb. 1619/20.
Under age in 1559
buried 7th Oct. 1613

Edward Lucas =
of Shillington
bapt. 16th Sept. 1585
Will dated 1st June 1650
proved 23rd May 1651

Edward Lucas = Elizabeth Knott, widow of Essenden
of Shillington   married at Essenden 28th Aug. 1642
Will dated 18th Oct. 1693   buried 18th Feb. 1676/7 at Hitchin.

William Lucas I = Mary, dau. of Thomas and Frances Field
of Hitchin   buried 29th Jan. 1679/80.
Will dated 6th Nov. 1704
proved 1706

William Lucas II = Sarah Rudd of Cottered
b. 1675, d. 1748   d. 1771.

William Lucas III = Phoebe Gray of London.
Brewer, Hitchin
b. 1710, d. 1751

William Lucas IV = 1st Sarah Redman of Earith, 2nd Susanna
Brewer, Hitchin   Camps.
b. 1744, d. 1819

William Lucas V = Ann Bowly of Cirencester
Brewer, Hitchin   b. 8th Sept. 1769, m. 15th Nov. 1798
b. in Sun St. 1768   d. 1853.
d. 1846

William Lucas VI = Eliza Clay, daughter of Wm. Clay, London
Brewer, Hitchin   b. 1802, m. 1830, d. 1898.
b. Tilehouse, Hitchin, 1804
d. Wratten, Hitchin, 1861

Appendix B

Phebe Family Tree

Introduction to Phebe's Family Trees

The following six pages contain representations of the family trees appended by Phebe to her Recollections. For reference purposes, they have been entitled Family Tree 1 to 6. The diagrams are a re-creation of those as set down by Phebe in her journal and no changes have been made to the original information provided by her, apart from highlighting the names of the family for whom additional information has been included in the Biographical Details in Chapter 6. In summary, the trees contain the following family information:

Family Tree 1

> **Top:** William Lucas IV and Sarah Redman (Phebe's Great Grandparents) + William's 2nd wife Susannah Camps and children.
> **Bottom:** Phebe's Aunt and Uncle – Phebe and Samuel Allen and children.

Family Tree 2

> **Top:** Phebe's immediate parental family and the children and grandchildren of her eldest brother, Joseph.
> **Bottom:** The family of Phebe's niece, Hannah Louisa Hayward (née Lucas).

Family Tree 3

> **Top:** Phebe's brother Edward and descendents.
> **Bottom:** Edward's daughter Lucy Penney and children.

Family Tree 4

> The descendants of Emma and Thomas Woolston Lucas.

Family Tree 5

> The descendants of Christiana and Jeffery Lucas.

Family Tree 6

> Phebe and Thomas Glaisyer and descendants.

Family Tree 1

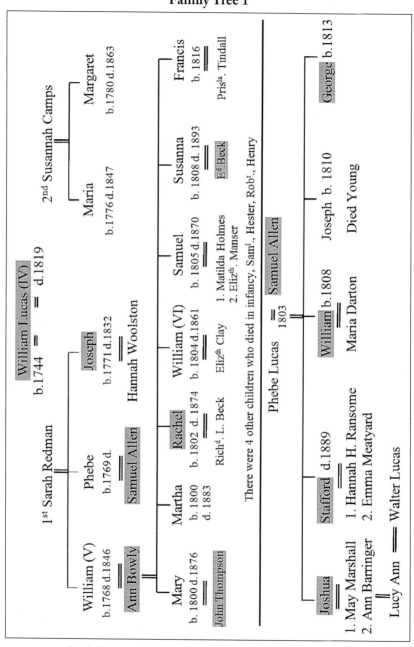

Sarah (Redman) and William Lucas were Phebe's grandparents.

Family Tree 2

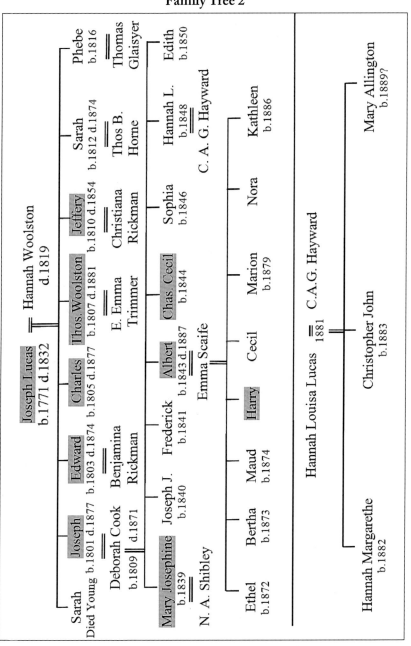

Family Tree 3

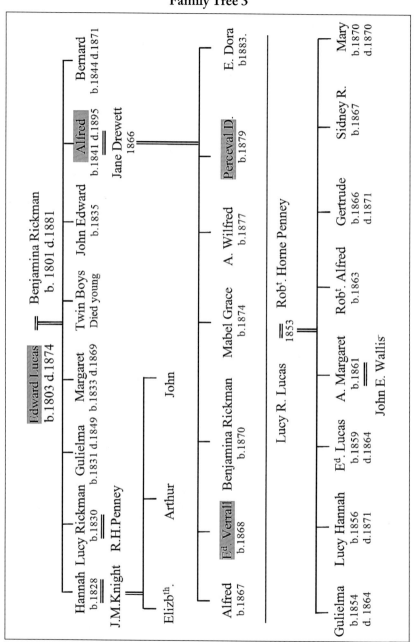

Edward Lucas was Phebe's brother.

Family Tree 4

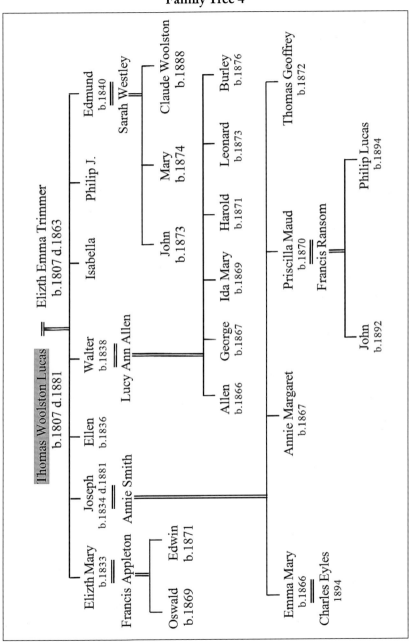

Thomas Woolston Lucas was Phebe's brother.

Family Tree 5

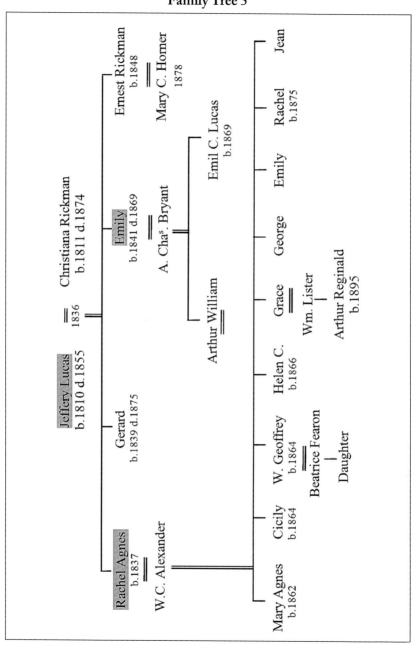

Jeffery Lucas was Phebe's brother.

Family Tree 6

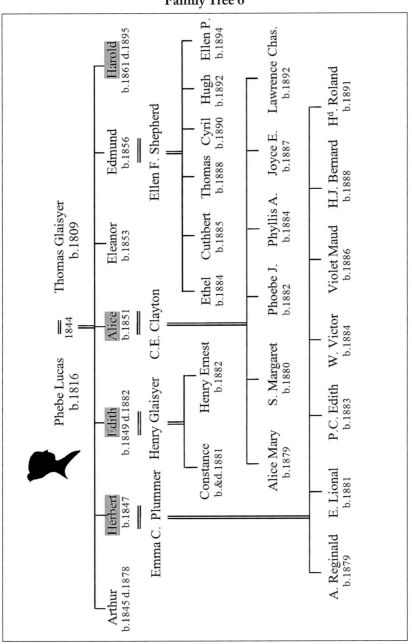

Appendix C

Probate of Will of Joseph Lucas

(Phebe's Father)

Copy probate of will of 24 May 1828 of Joseph Lucas prepared by C.C.Lucas of 1 Trinity Place, Charing Cross, London

— to his friends William Brown of Hitchin [Hertfordshire], baker, William Exton of Grove Mill, Hitchin, banker and Joseph Sharples of Hitchin, gentleman as trustees for sale — his piece of freehold land in Ippollittes [Hertfordshire] in occupation of Abraham Folls; one freehold and two copyhold lots of farm pasture adjoining each other in Brackhill Farm, Earith [Huntingdonshire] in occupation of George Purchase; real and personal estate at Pirton [Hertfordshire] in occupation of Mary, widow of William Hodson and John Weedon;

— to his friends William Brown, William Exton and Joseph Sharples as trustees for sale — half the freehold estates owned by he and his brother William, both purchased by them and devised them by their father as tenants in common (his brother agreeing to release the testator's half share after the testator's death);

— to his friends William Brown, William Exton and Joseph Sharples £50 each provided they act as trustees;

— to Sarah Woolston ("now living with me") £50;

— to Thomas Marsh, his clerk, £50;

— to John Lenton, his servant at Offley Grange, £10;

— to William Hunt the elder, Francis Smith the elder and George Westwood £10 each;

— Mary Valentine and Sarah Pack, his household servants £10 each;

— to his sons Joseph, Charles, Thomas Woolston and Jeffery £1,500 each;

— to his son Edward £500 (he already having had £1,000);

— to his daughters Sarah and Phebe £1,000 each;[96]

— to his son Joseph the mahogany wardrobe in his own use, his encyclopaedia, concordance and family Bible;

— to Sarah and Phebe the remainder of the books, household furniture, plate, linen, china etc.;

— residue of personal estate to William Brown, William Exton and Joseph Sharples upon trust;

— residue of personal estate and money from sales of land, after debts and legacies above, to be shared equally between his seven children Joseph, Edward, Charles, Thomas Woolston, Jeffery, Sarah and Phebe, William

---

[96] Approximately £75,000 by current values using the Retail Price Index for comparison.

Brown, William Exton and Joseph Sharples acting as guardians for his children under 21

— witnesses: Thomas Barton Beck of Hitchin, gentleman, Robert Bloome of Hitchin, cooper and Thomas Davies of Hitchin, painter

Affidavit of 13 Jan 1833 of Stafford Allen of 8 Cowper Street, Old Street Road [Middlesex] that: he was a Quaker; he knew Joseph Lucas for several years before his death and recognised his handwriting in his will as genuine especially in relation to the pencilling in of the names of William Brown, William Exton and Joseph Sharples . Affidavit of 4 Feb 1833 of John Thompson of Hitchin, draper, also a Quaker, affirming the same as Stafford Allen

Probate in PCC (Prerogative Court of Canterbury) 7 Feb 1833

A display at Hitchin Museum, showing various brewery artefacts, including Lucas company beverage containers. Photographed by the author in 2004

Sources and Recommended Reading

A Quaker Journal: Being the Diary and Reminiscences of William Lucas — Edited by G. E. Bryant & G. P. Baker. Published by Hutchinson & Co. Ltd., 1933 (Two Volumes)

A Suppressed Cry – Victoria Glendenning. Published by Routledge & Kegan Paul Ltd, 1969. SBN: 7100 6460 8

Brewers In Hertfordshire – By Allan Whitaker. Published by the University of Hertfordshire Press, 2006. ISBN: 0—9542189—7—3

D. H. Lawrence, 1885—1930: The Cambridge Biography — By David Ellis, John Worthen, Mark Kinkead—Weekes. Published by Cambridge University Press, 1996 ISBN: 0521254205, 9780521254205. Now published on the internet by Google Book Search.

E. V. Lucas: A Portrait – By Audrey Lucas. Published by Methuen & Co. Ltd., 1939

Exploring Hitchin: A virtual walk around Hitchin. A compact disc produced in 2006 by Hitchin Historical Society.

Family Fragments: respecting the ancestry, acquaintance and marriage of Richard Low Beck and Rachel Lucas — Privately published by William Beck in 1897. Now published on the internet by The Family History Archives: *http://www.lib.byu.edu/online.html*

Friends in Bedfordshire and West Hertfordshire — By Joyce Godber. Published by Joyce Godber, 1975

Hertfordshire Archive — a digital archive of past publications about Hertfordshire:
Hertfordshire's Past — Issue 02 — Spring 1977 — Evidence of Literacy from the Muster Roll of the Hitchin Volunteer Corps of 1803—09: *http://www.hertfordshire—archive.co.uk/*

Hitchin British Schools, Schooldays, Booklet No 2 – By Fiona Dodwell. Published by North Hertfordshire District Council, 1993. ISBN: 0902755 04 8

Hitchin Quakers Ancient & Modern A transcript of a Talk by Metford Robson Given to Hitchin Historical Society in November 2002.

Hitchin Worthies – By Reginald L. Hine F.S.A F.R.Hist.S. First published by Eric T. More. Republished 1974. ISBN: 0 9502391 1 9

People, Places and Past Times of Hitchin Written and published by E Aillie Latchmore, 1974

Quakers In Lewes, An Informal History – By David Hitchin. Published by Lewes Quakers, 1984.

Recollections of Hitchin as relayed by Matilda Lucas (1849—1943) to Reginald Hine in 1930 – Hitchin Museum

The Book of Hitchin – By Anthony M. Foster. Published by Barracuda Books Ltd. 1981. ISBN: 0 86023 13 0

The Development of Education in Hitchin 1780—1880 by K.R.J. Aitken B.A. A thesis submitted for an M.A. degree, May 1960. Typescript document held by Hitchin Museum.

The Diary of Joshua Whiting – Compiled by Sarah Graham. Published by William Sessions Ltd, 2006. The Ebor Press York. ISBN: 1 85072 318 4

The History of Hitchin – By Reginald L. Hine F.S.A F.R.Hist.S. Published by George Allen & Unwin Ltd., 1927/1929. (Two Volumes)

The Old Contemporaries – By E.V. Lucas. Published by Methuen & Co. Ltd., 1935

The Sea Voyages of Edward Beck in the 1820s' – Kenneth M. Hay & Joy Roberts. Published by the Pentland Press Ltd. ISBN: 1 85821 435 1

Take The Train From Hitchin – By Phil Howard. Published by Hitchin Historical Society, 2006. ISBN 0—9552411—03

Sketches Of Rural Life And Other Poems — By Francis Lucas. First Published in 1889 by Macmillan & Co. Now published by Kessinger Publishing's Rare Reprints (A print 'on—demand' service) Internet: *WWW.kessinger.net*. ISBN: 143706275X 9 781437 062755

Various Lucas family papers in the care of Hitchin Museum.

Various Quaker records in the care of East Sussex County Records Office, Lewes.

A plaque preserved in the archway leading to the yard of The Tilehouse, in Tilehouse Street, Hitchin. It reads "The whole length of this wall and down to the cellar floor of the adjoining house belongs to William Lucas. Rebuilt 1821". Photographed by Scilla Douglas 1995.

INDEX

PEOPLE

Alexander, Mary Agnes (May)   68, 96
Alexander, Rachel Agnes
   (née Lucas)   68, 69, 83, 96
Alexander, William Cleverly   68, 69, 96
Allen, Ann (née Barringer)   69, 92
Allen, Emma (née Meatyard)   71, 92
Allen, George   69, 92
Allen, Hannah (née Ransome)   71, 92
Allen, Joseph   49, 92
Allen, Joshua   49, 92
Allen, Maria (née Darton)   71, 92
Allen, Mary (née Marshall)   69, 92
Allen, Phebe (née Lucas)
   23, 24, 31, 45, 46, 47, 48, 49, 50, 51,
   55, 56, 62, 65, 66, 69, 70, 71, 91, 92
Allen, Samuel   9, 23, 24, 45, 48, 50, 62,
   66, 69, 70, 71, 91, 92
Allen, Stafford   48, 71, 92, 99
Allen, William   49, 71, 92
Allen, William FRS, FLS
   (Philanthropist)   49, 70
Ansell, Edward   23
Ansell, Thomas   23
Arnold, Mathew   28
Atkins (Butcher in Cock Street)   25, 40
Audley, George   15

Barham, C. Loftus   15
Barrie, James Mathew
   (Sir, 1st Baronet, OM)   82
Barton, Bernard (The Quaker Poet)   82
Bass, Isaac   12, 33, 58, 59, 63, 72, 81
Bass, Isaac Gray   58, 60
Bass, Sarah
   (née Glaisyer)   58, 60, 72, 75, 81
Beaver, George (Hitchin Surveyor)   24
Beck, Edward   56, 72, 73, 92, 101
Beck, Jane (née Morris)   72, 73, 92
Beck, Rachel (née Lucas)2, 53, 71, 73, 92
Beck, Richard Low
   71, 72, 73, 74, 75, 92, 100
Beck, Susanna (née Lucas)
   53, 54, 56, 62, 64, 70, 72, 92
Binks, Mary (née Woolston)   59, 74, 75
Binks, William   74

Bowly, Samuel   19
Bowman, Ernest
   (Miller at Westmill)   24
Bowyer, William (Wife of)   24
Brown, William   57, 98, 99
Bryant, Arthur Charles   76, 96
Bryant, Elizabeth (née Lucas)   76, 85
Bryant, Emily (née Lucas)   76, 83, 96
Bunyan, John   6
Burr, Edward
   (Teddy – Miller at Charlton)   36, 37
Burr, Mary (of Charlton Mill)   36
Burr, Thomas (Brewer of Dunstable)   17

Chapman, George (dramatist)   51
Child, William (Brewer & Cooper)   18
Clayton, Alice (née Glaisyer)   66, 76, 97
Clayton, Alice Mary   97
Clayton, Charles   76, 97
Clayton, Joyce E.   97
Clayton, Lawrence Charles   iv, 35, 97
Clayton, Pheobe J.   97
Clayton, Phyllis A.   97
Clayton, S. Margaret   97
Collins, Benjamin Bull   49
Conquest, Elizabeth   14
Conquest, William   14
Cook, William (Malt Maker)   18
Cowper, William (Poet)   34, 48
Cox, William   24
Crosse (Mrs – Schoolmistress in
   Hitchin)   40, 41
Crosse, Kate   40
Crouch (Miss
   – Schoolmistress in Hitchin)   61

Dimsdale, John   76
Draper, Ann   14
Draper, Edward   15
Draper, John   8, 14
Drewett, Joseph (Co-founder of
   Woodlands School)   79
Dunnage, John   17

Exton, Mary (née Ransom)   41, 42
Exton, William   41, 98, 99

Foster, Henrietta 59
Foster, Jane 59
Foster, Mary 59
Foster, Oswald (Doctor – Jnr) 10, 59
Foster, Oswald
   (Doctor – Snr) 31, 43, 76, 85
Fox, George 5, 6
Fry, Elizabeth (née Gurney) 13

Glaisyer, A. Reginald 12, 77, 97
Glaisyer, Arthur 97
Glaisyer, Constance 77, 97
Glaisyer, Cuthbert 97
Glaisyer, Cyril 97
Glaisyer, E. Lional 97
Glaisyer, Edith (née Glaisyer) 77, 97
Glaisyer, Edmund 66, 97
Glaisyer, Eleanor 66, 97
Glaisyer, Elizabeth (Bessy) 59
Glaisyer, Elizabeth
   (née Rickman) 63, 75, 81
Glaisyer, Ellen (née Wright) 42
Glaisyer, Ellen F. (née Shepherd) 97
Glaisyer, Ellen P. 97
Glaisyer, Emma C. (née Plummer) 77, 97
Glaisyer, Ethel 97
Glaisyer, Harold 77, 97
Glaisyer, Harold Roland 97
Glaisyer, Henry 77, 97
Glaisyer, Henry Ernest 77, 97
Glaisyer, Herbert 66, 77, 97
Glaisyer, Herbert J. Bernard 97
Glaisyer, Hugh 97
Glaisyer, John 58, 80
Glaisyer, Joseph 42
Glaisyer, P.C. Edith 97
Glaisyer, Thomas
   (b.1809) iv, 62, 66, 77, 91, 97
Glaisyer, Thomas (b.1888) 97
Glaisyer, Violet Maud 97
Glaisyer, W. Victor 77, 97
Godlee, Ann 64, 65
Godlee, Lucy 65
Godlee, Mary (née Rickman) 65
Godlee, Rebecca 65
Gray, Isaac 14, 16
Gray, John 12

Haydon, Benjamin Robert (Artist) 71

Hayward, Hannah Louisa
   (née Lucas) 91, 93
Hine, Reginald iv, 5, 7, 10, 15, 19,
   28, 68, 71, 80, 87, 89, 100, 101
Hobbs, Henry 8
Hobbs, William 8
Horne, John 87
Horne, Sarah (née Lucas
   – Phebe's sister) 32, 33, 37, 40, 41,
   42, 45, 56, 59, 61, 62, 63, 64, 65, 93, 98
Horne, Thomas Benjamin 65, 93
Hudson (Miss – Schoolmistress
   in Hitchin) 61

Jeeves, Emma 20
Jeeves, John 20, 38
Jermyn (Family) 89
Jermyn, Henry 57
Jervis (Brewery Worker) 40

Kemp, Mina 59
Kilby, John 8
Knight, Hannah (née Lucas) 65, 94
Knight, John Messer 65, 94

Lamb, Charles 82, 83
Latchmore, Edward 9
Law, William (ex-Lucas Malt Maker) 18
Lawrence David Herbert Richards
   (D.H.) 85, 100
Lax, William The Revd. Professor 36
Leadbeater, Mary (Childrens' author) 48
Lenton, John (Baliff at
   Offley Grange) 35, 98
Lewis, V, Miss (Last owner
   of Perks Shop) 25
Lidbetter, Ann (née Woolston) 59, 74
Lidbetter, Thomas 59, 74
Lister, Grace (née Alexander) 68, 96
Lister, Joseph Jackson 73, 74
Lucas, Albert 78, 93
Lucas, Albert Henry (Harry) 78, 79, 93
Lucas, Alfred (1841-1895) 79, 81, 84, 94
Lucas, Alice 51
Lucas, Alice (née ??) 90
Lucas, Ann (née Bowly) 2, 19, 31, 33,
   53, 55, 56, 61, 65, 72, 80, 85, 89, 92
Lucas, Annie (née Smith) 51, 95
Lucas, Audrey 79, 82, 83, 100
Lucas, Benjamina (née Rickman)
   60, 63, 64, 65, 79, 81, 94

Lucas, Charles 32, 33, 59, 80, 93, 98
Lucas, Charles Cecil 80, 93
Lucas, Christiana (née Rickman)
63, 68, 76, 91, 93, 96
Lucas, Deborah (née Cooke) 78, 84, 93
Lucas, Edith (née Speares) 78, 79
Lucas, Edward (1585-1650) 23, 90
Lucas, Edward (1693) 90
Lucas, Edward (1803-1874)
23, 32, 33, 58, 59, 60, 62, 63, 64,
65, 79, 80, 81, 91, 93, 94, 98
Lucas, Edward Verrell
7, 76, 79, 81, 82, 84, 94, 101
Lucas, Elizabeth (née Clay) 76, 90, 92
Lucas, Elizabeth Emma
(née Trimmer) 60, 85, 91, 95
Lucas, Emma Eliza Wilhelmina
(née Scaife) 78, 93
Lucas, Florence Elizabeth
(née Griffiths) 82
Lucas, Francis 19, 43, 44, 53, 65, 66,
68, 70, 76, 87, 92, 101
Lucas, Hannah (née Woolston)
12, 16, 32, 33, 45, 65, 81, 83, 84, 93
Lucas, Ida Mary 9, 95
Lucas, Jane (née Drewett) 79, 81, 84, 94
Lucas, Jeffery 32, 33, 62, 63, 74,
83, 93, 96, 98
Lucas, John (d. circa 1559) 90
Lucas, John (of Tooting) 60
Lucas, John Albert 78
Lucas, Joseph (1771-1832) 9, 16, 18,
31, 32, 33, 35, 36, 39, 42, 49, 54, 55,
56, 57, 61, 62, 65, 83, 84, 86, 92, 93
Lucas, Joseph (1801-1877) 10, 11, 18,
19, 20, 32, 33, 42, 78, 84, 93, 98
Lucas, Madeleine (née Meynell) 84
Lucas, Margaret
(1780-1863) 51, 52, 53, 92
Lucas, Maria 51, 52, 53, 92
Lucas, Martha 33, 36, 92
Lucas, Mary (née Field) 90
Lucas, Matilda 7, 10, 11, 19, 25,
26, 28, 84, 89, 101
Lucas, Olive Beatrice 78
Lucas, Perceval Drewett 82, 83, 84, 94
Lucas, Phebe (née Gray)
14, 15, 31, 86, 90
Lucas, Richard 23, 90

Lucas, Samuel (Jnr) 20, 84
Lucas, Samuel (Snr) 7, 13, 18, 53, 68, 92
Lucas, Sarah (1800-1801) 2, 93
Lucas, Sarah (née Redman) 50, 86, 91, 92
Lucas, Stephen 21
Lucas, Susannah
(née Camps) 14, 51, 85, 86, 92
Lucas, Sylvia 84, 85
Lucas, Thomas Woolston
32, 33, 60, 61, 85, 91, 93, 95
Lucas, Walter (b. 1898) 11
Lucas, William (Miller at Shotling
- alive in 1613) 41
Lucas, William I 7, 25, 90
Lucas, William II 8, 14, 90
Lucas, William III 12, 14, 15, 86, 90
Lucas, William IV
14, 16, 49, 50, 51, 83, 86, 91, 92
Lucas, William V 2, 9, 11, 16, 17, 18,
19, 24, 25, 27, 31, 33, 35, 39, 42, 43,
44, 49, 53, 54, 55, 56, 57, 68, 71, 72,
73, 76, 80, 83, 86, 89, 90, 92, 98
Lucas, William VI
1, 2, 4, 10, 11, 13, 18, 19, 24, 53, 68,
70, 71, 73, 74, 75, 76, 80, 83, 90, 92
Lucas, William VII 20, 21, 22, 90
Lucas, William VIII 90
Lytton, Lord 28

Marsh, Eliza 33, 42
Marsh, Thomas 17, 18, 33, 38, 57, 98
May, Ann 62, 66, 85
May, Charles 71
May, Samuel 62, 83
Meynell, Alice (née Thompson) 84
Meynell, Wilfred 84
Milne, Alan Alexander (Author) 82
Moule, Alice (née Foster) 10

Nash, John (Architect) 4
Newton, John (Revd.) 34
Newton, Robert 57
Niblock, Amelia St. John 87
Niblock, Joseph White (Rev. Dr.
- of Hitchin Free School) 32, 86, 87

Osborn, George (Brewey worker) 18
Owen, Robert 1

Pack, Sarah 33, 37, 98
Papworth, John (Alias Bradwell) 23

Peckover Mrs. Alexr. 41
Peckover, Alexander
(1st Baron Peckover) 41
Penney, Lucy Rickman (née Lucas) 91, 94
Penney, Robert Horne 81, 94
Pollard, Joseph 88
Prince Regent, The 1, 3, 4, 53

Queen Anne 31

Radcliffe, Ralph 6, 7
Randall (Family) 26
Ransom, Ernestine 43
Ransom, Esther (née Whiting 9, 42, 43
Ransom, John (1749-1828) 42, 95
Ransom, Joseph 8, 40, 41
Ransom, Joseph (Alive In 1723) 8
Ransom, Maria 43
Ransom, William (Executor of
Jos. Lucas Jnr Estate) 88
Read, Ann 33
Read, Mary 33
Reynolds, Fanny (Schoolmistress in
Tilehouse Street) 40
Rickman, Emily 59, 60, 64, 65
Rickman, John 12, 63, 64, 81, 87, 88
Rickman, Priscilla 64
Rickman, Sarah (née Horne) 63, 87
Rudd, Sarah 90

Sanders, Joseph 8
Saunders, R 22
Scarborough, Christopher
(Lucas Brewery Agent) 20
Scott, Walter (Sir) 49, 59
Seebohm, Frederick 40
Sexton, William (Brewer) 17
Sharples, Elizabeth (née Ransom) 41, 42
Sharples, Joseph 8, 36, 41, 88, 98, 99
Shibley, Mary Josephine
(née Lucas) 88, 93
Shibley, Nassib Abdullah 88, 93
Smith, Ann (of Olney) 48
Smith, Frank (Brewery Gardener) 39, 98
Smith, Mary (of Olney) 48
Smyth, Hugh 22
Snow, John (of Brighton) 74
Spavold, Samuel 15, 16
Spencer, Daniel 15
Spring-Rice, Bernard 69

Spring-Rice, Cicely
(née Alexander) 68, 69, 96
Squire, Thomas 86
Strange, Priscilla (née May) 62
Taylor, Ann 34
Taylor, George
(Lucas Brewery Manager) 20
Taylor, Jane 34
Taylor, W. C. (Lucas Brewery agent) 20
Thompson, Catherine 89
Thompson, James 58
Thompson, John 10, 25, 26, 27, 28,
33, 40, 89, 92, 99
Thompson, Lawson 28, 66, 89
Thompson, Margaret 28, 89
Thompson, Mary 28, 89
Thompson, Mary (née Lucas)
25, 27, 33, 36, 40, 53, 89, 92
Thompson, Sarah
(Sally – née Bass) 58, 59
Trimmer, Sarah (Author) 52
Tuke, Esther 12, 32
Tuke, James Hack 79
Turner, John 8

Valentine, Mary (Brewery
House cook) 37, 38, 55, 98
Vanderbilt Family 77

Waddington, Debby
(Nursemaid to Sally Bass) 58
Watts, Isaac (Dr) 47
Western, H G 23
Westwood, George (Brewer) 18, 39, 98
Wheeler, Elizabeth 62, 66
Whistler, James 68, 69
Whiting, John 10, 19, 42
Whiting, Joshua 9, 101
Whiting, Margaret 42
Whiting, Mary 42
Whittingstall, James 23
Wiblow, John 60, 85
Wiblow, Mary 60
Wiles, Henry (Revd.) 2
Wiles, Sarah 56, 57
Wilkinson, Thomas 49
William & Mary, (King & Queen) 7
Woolston, Sarah (Phebe's
Cousin) 33, 34, 59, 61, 64, 74, 98

Selected Events, Places and Things

Abbeville (The Somme)　　　　85
American Friends' Service Committee 13
Ampthill　　　62, 66, 69, 71, 73, 83
Anti-Vaccination League　　　79

Baldock　　　　　　5, 7, 11, 89
Battencourt Château, The Marne　82
Brighton Chain Pier　　　　60
Brighton Place
　(Isaac Bass residence)　　58, 60
Brighton Royal Pavillion　　　4
Brighton, Buckingham Road　　80
Brighton, York Place, (No 18
　– Phebe's 1st home in Brighton)　66
British & Foreign Bible Society　28
British Library　　　　　　81
Bryant & May
　Match Company　　12, 76, 83
Burlington Fine Arts Club　　68

Casebourne & Lucas
　(Cement Manufacturers)　　78
Child/Infant Mortality　　　2
Cholera　　　　　　　2, 18
Coalbrookdale Foundary　　　12
Commonwealth Government　　5
Corballis Castle, Rathdrum,
　Co. Wicklow　　　　　　78
Corn Laws, The　　　　　1
Court Leet　　　　　　　15

Declaration of Indulgence　　7
Disownment (from The Society
　of Friends)　　　　　6, 75
Distraint　　　　　　　6, 7
Downe House　　　　　　82
Drayton-in-the-Clay, Leicestershire　5

Elgin Marbles, The　　　　4

Friends' Birth Record – Phebe Lucas　31
Friends' Burial Ground: Black Rock　66
Friends' Burial Ground: Hitchin
　8, 9, 10, 50, 71, 76, 80, 83, 84, 89
Friends' Burial Ground: Horsham　75
Friends' Burial Ground: Isleworth　72
Friends' Burial Ground: St. Ibbs　8

Friends' Burial Ground:
　Stoke Newington　　　71, 74
Friends' Meeting House: Arundel　87
Friends' Meeting House: Cirencester　80
Friends' Meeting House: Cranfield　69
Friends' Meeting House: Esher　76
Friends' Meeting House: Finedon　83
Friends' Meeting House: Guildford　85
Friends' Meeting House: Hertford　7
Friends' Meeting House: Hitchin
　8, 9, 10, 11, 13, 25, 50, 66, 70, 71, 73
Friends' Meeting House: Ipswich　71
Friends' Meeting House: Lewes
　　　　　　　　63, 64, 81, 83
Friends' Meeting House: Luton　65
Friends' Meeting House: St Ives　86
Friends' Meeting House:
　Wellingborough　　　　74, 84
Friends' Meeting House:
　Woburn Sands　　　　　79
Friends' School: Ackworth, Pontefract
　　　　　　　　12, 32, 79, 81
Friends' School: Armstrong School:
　Doncaster　　　　　　2, 73
Friends' School: Compton, Dorset　89
Friends' School: Epping　　　33
Friends' School: Grove House,
　Tottenham　　　　　41, 80, 86
Friends' School: Hemel Hempstead　86
Friends' School: Lewes　　　65
Friends' School: Thornaby-on-Tees　78
Friends' School: York Girls'
　(Esther Tuke)　　　　　32
Friends' Service Council　　　13

General Pardon, The　　　　7
Glaisyer & Kemp, Apothecaries,
　Brighton　　　　　　33, 66
Graham Ranger Beauty Salon　22
Great Northern Railway　　　3
Green, J. W. (Brewers of Luton)　21, 22
Guildford　　　　　　　60, 85

Hawley, Clay County, Minnesota　12, 77
Hertford　　　　　　　5, 7
Hertfordshire Monthly Meeting　7
Hitchin: Acorn Estate Agents　22

Hitchin: Arcade 4
Hitchin: Bancroft 40, 66, 68, 70, 76, 79
Hitchin: Barclays Bank
(and forerunners) 8, 12, 79, 81, 83, 88
Hitchin: Bedford Road 28, 43, 90
Hitchin: Brand Street 8, 28
Hitchin: Brewer's House,
Bridge Street 20, 38
Hitchin: Brewery House, Sun Street
iv, v, 15, 16, 17, 20, 22, 30, 31, 32,
34, 35, 37, 38, 39, 78, 80, 83, 84, 86
Hitchin: Bridge Street
15, 17, 19, 20, 22, 38
Hitchin: British School 56
Hitchin: Butts Close 10, 27, 28
Hitchin: Café Rouge 25, 28, 37, 39
Hitchin: Charlton Mill 36
Hitchin: Cock Street/High Street
4, 7, 10, 23, 25, 26, 27, 28, 39, 66, 89
Hitchin: Cooper's Arms 44
Hitchin: Crown House
(Inland Revenue) 22
Hitchin: Dead Street
/Queen Street 19, 56
Hitchin: Elmside House 28, 89
Hitchin: Free School 32, 86
Hitchin: gas company 4
Hitchin: Gatward,
Jewellers and Silversmiths 7
Hitchin: Jermyn Draper's Shop 25, 89
Hitchin: Loyal
Volunteer Association 17, 100
Hitchin: Manor Court Book 8, 23
Hitchin: Market Place 3, 7, 23
Hitchin: Mount Pleasant 42, 44
Hitchin: Natwest Bank 25
Hitchin: Philpotts Furnishers,
Sun Street v, 22
Hitchin: Railway Station 3
Hitchin: Regent Cottage Restaurant 25
Hitchin: Sales Motor Garage,
Bridge Street 22
Hitchin: St Mary's Church 2
Hitchin: Sun Street/Angel Street
iv, 14, 15, 16, 17, 22, 34, 35, 70, 80, 84
Hitchin: Swan Inn 3, 4
Hitchin: The Firs Hotel 90
Hitchin: Tilehouse Street 7, 16, 17, 22,
35, 40, 43, 44, 51, 53, 57, 73, 86, 101

Hitchin: Town Hall v, 9, 19
Hitchin: West Lane
/Payne's Park 13, 25, 29, 69, 70
Hitchin: Western House 16, 51
Hitchin: Woodlands School 79
Hiz, River 15, 16, 19, 23, 38

Ickleford 23, 45
Industrial Revolution, The 3
Irchester 84
Irthlingborough 32, 83

Kershaw Coach 3, 4
Kingshott School, St Ippollites 20, 84

Lawson Thompson scrapbook
(Hitchin Museum)
8, 20, 21, 24, 26, 41, 44, 55, 84, 87, 89
Leighton Buzzard 69, 70, 71
Lewes and Chichester
Monthly Meeting 66, 72, 75, 80, 81
Lewes, Bear Brewery 87
Lindfield Rural Colony 49
London Road, Brighton (No 96
– Phebe's family home) 66
Long Depression, The 1
Lucas, Samuel
– Paintings & Drawings ii, 11, 15,
36, 37, 45, 48, 54, 57, 67, 70, 71, 75, 80

Malting 14, 19, 25, 28, 33, 40, 87
Mill Hill School 84, 85

National Portrait Gallery, The 71
Nobel Peace Prize 13

Oak Hill Lodge,
Kingston-upon-Thames 76
Oakfield House,
St Ippollittes 11, 20, 80, 84
Oaklands Farm, Crowborough 79
Offley Grange 35, 98

Pall Mall Gallery, The 69
Park Street, Luton 79
Perks & Llewellyn
(Chemist & Lavender Co.) 25
Peterloo Massacre, The 1
Population, Hitchin: 2

Quaker Act, 1662 6
Quaker Calendar iv
Quaker Sampler 46, 61

Rathdrum, County Wicklow   78, 79
Regency England   v, 1, 3
River Oughton (Orton)
  & Oughtonhead   23, 44, 48
RMS Adriatic (White Star Line)   77
RMS Bothnia (Cunard Line)   77
Royal Pharmaceutical Society, The 49

Salisbury & Winchester Journal, The 74
Salvation Army   79
Scarlet Fever   73
Sedbergh (Cumbria)   5
Sheringham, Norfolk   78
Shillington   23
Shotling/Burnt/Grove Mill   41, 98
Slavery, Abolition of 13, 48, 49, 68, 70, 71
Smallpox   32, 50, 70, 85
Southwick, Sussex   59, 64, 74, 79, 81
Stamford Hill   74
Stanegarth (Westmorland)   7
Stockton & Darlington Railway   3, 12
Stranton Parish Church, Hartlepool 78

Tate Gallery, The   69
Taxidermy   48, 61, 62, 80
Temperance & Abstinence   19, 79
Thornton-le-Moor, Yorkshire   78
Tokenhouse Yard, City of London   74
Toleration Act   7
Tooting   60
Tower Hamlets   70
Travelling Ministers   15, 16, 70
Tyburn   12
Typhus   2, 73

Walsworth   23
Waterloo, Battle of   1, 8

A disused safe survives at the Brewery House.
Photographed by the author, by courtesy of
Christine Low and Matthew Philpott.

Wellingham House, Lewes
                  59, 63, 64, 65, 83, 87
West Mill   23, 24, 45, 47, 48, 69, 70, 71
Wolstanbury, Sussex   45
Woodham Ferrers   70
Woodingdean, Lawn
  Memorial Cemetery   66

Hitchin Historical Society

The Society aims to increase and spread knowledge of the history of Hitchin, and is a registered charity. We hold regular meetings on the fourth Thursday of most months and arrange visits to local buildings and institutions, many of which are not normally open to the general public. We also organize trips to places of historical interest further afield. Members receive a regular newsletter and magazine, the Hitchin Journal. The Society also produces high-quality publications on the history of the town based on research into the origins and development of buildings, organizations, crafts, trades and other aspects of historical interest.